NATURAL CONSEQUENCES

Intimate Essays for a Planet in Peril

NATURAL CONSEQUENCES

Intimate Essays for a Planet in Peril

CHAR MILLER

REVERBERATIONS BOOKS

Publisher
Reverberations Books
Santa Cruz, CA
www.reverberationsbooks.com

Imprint of Chin Music Press
Seattle, WA
www.chinmusicpress.com

Library of Congress Control Number:
2022935659
ISBN: 978-1-63405-037-1

First Edition
Printed in Canada

For Heili and Nora

ACKNOWLEDGEMENTS

Natural Consequences has benefitted greatly from travels and conversations with my comrade-in-arms Judi Lipsett, whose insights and editorial interventions have been crucial to this book and all others. Susan Brenneman at the *Los Angeles Times,* and for whom some of these essays were initially written, has sharpened my prose and pushed for greater nuance in it. At Reverberations Books/Chin Music Press I am indebted to publishers Gregory Graalfs and Bruce Rutledge for their enthusiasm, generosity, and support. And a major shout out to friend and colleague Todd Shimoda: He read every word of *Natural Consequences* and made it much tighter and more compelling.

As this book went into production, two major life events occurred within my extended family. In late December 2021, our daughter and son-in-law brought the amazing Elinor Ruth (Nora) into this world. Five days later, after cheering Nora's birth, my beloved sister, Heili, died. *Natural Consequences* is dedicated to them, and the inescapable weave of love and loss, joy and grief.

CONTENTS

POINTS OF DEPARTURE

Utah, Sepulveda links colonial-settler society's efforts to displace the region's Indigenous Peoples and the landscape they stewarded with its intense efforts to control the Santa Ana River. Channeled, dammed, and leveed, the river has been desecrated. Yet to restore the region's largest watershed requires more than dismantling its concrete-straightjacketed condition that defines its once-braided course. "I want to bring her back to life and decolonize our sacred waters," he writes, by exposing the "colonial processes through the history of systematic domestication forced on both Native peoples and their lands/waters" and to develop an "alternative model meant to assist in the re-establishment of human-beings' organic relationships to land." Central here is the concept of Kuuyam, the Tongva word for guests. By this means, non-natives are "potential guests of the tribal people, and more importantly—of the land itself." The land as place not only is sanctified, it's replete with life "beyond human interests."

It's one thing to acknowledge that the settler society of which I am a part has brutalized and dispossessed Indigenous Peoples while exploiting the land, its soils, minerals, and waters. It's another thing to figure out how to live and act as a good guest. My instinct—and *Natural Consequences* is an outgrowth of it—is to start small. To observe, to witness, to reflect. To wonder. Then to write about the things that catch my eye or that I don't understand yet feel the need to, and frame these inchoate thoughts, as historians tend to do, in context. Our professional conceit is straightforward—the past matters. But to what degree? To whom and for whom? Why? There are no simple answers to these questions, and one could spend a lifetime trying to come to terms with them. Trust me, I have. The process only gets more complicated if the claim that the past matters is made relative to environmental politics and policy. Those who formulate policy at all levels of government tend to do so reactively — the goal is to solve a set of pre-existing concerns with relative dispatch. Historians are reflective; speed is not our concern. Nothing slows down the process like asking whether the problem as defined is in fact a problem, or asking if it's a problem only for those who have defined it. Is there another unidentified issue that might be more important to more people and for different reasons? You can see why we don't get invited out much.

So I have to wrangle any invitation I can to speak with land managers, wildland firefighters, and grassroots organizations committed to environmental preservation and justice; or those devoted to ecological restoration, urban greening, and watershed health; or any civic group or cultural institution — from the League of Women Voters and the Autry Museum to the Rotary Club. Ok, I'm an academic and talk for a living, so this impulse to get in front of a microphone isn't solely about public service. That said, most of the time the event's organizers offer ideas about of-the-moment topics and hot-button issues their constituencies wish to explore. Their ideas set the agenda, and I have to decipher as best I can how and why the requisite concerns have emerged, contextualizing their on-the-ground realities and historical underpinnings. If I'm lucky, the conversations do not end there, but might morph into a professional article, magazine essay, newspaper commentary, blog post, or even a book. *Natural Consequences* grew out of my engagements with these opportunities and the chances I've been given to speak to communities about the decisions earlier generations made for how they would live, work, and act in and on the world. My larger hope is that more informed deliberations about the past might lead to smarter choices for the future, though this too is a touch self-serving. Entering the civic arena, participating in public debate and discourse, engaging as an ally, and amplifying voices of those too-long silenced, may also help me and others become more thoughtful guests.

That the dominant culture—industrial, profit-driven, consuming—has been a rampaging visitor, that we have trashed this good earth, is evident in the issue-centered and site-specific chapters that follow. So are some of the possible resolutions, whether implied or explicit. If we are to understand our place in whatever location we inhabit, step one is to step out. Walking a street, strolling along rivers or even flood-control channels, hiking uphill and down, or playing in a park or on a beach—each offers a respite. The essays in *Re/creation* suggest outdoor activities can spark conversations about the physical terrain through which we move. It sparks ideas we might hold about our environment and how we might share them. This interplay and the context in which it occurs is what in *Camping Grounds* (2021) historian Phoebe Young calls "public nature," a setting "where people work out relationships to nature, nation, and each other."

How we develop a new relationship with wildfire, the subject of *Embers,* may determine the larger contours of life in California and other parts of the flammable West. That is why these essays read like dispatches from some hellish frontline. But the battle is not with fire as fire, although combat is often the rhetorical device that journalists and public officials deploy to describe the effort to control these blazes. The battle is with ourselves. It's with the historic decision the US Forest Service and other agencies made in the early twentieth century to suppress fire and, not incidentally, oppress Indigenous fire managers for whom the flame was a natural land-management tool. Conquering fire has been a particularly onerous form of racial imperialism. The consequences of those actions can be read in the intensifying wildfires in the first decades of the twenty-first century, conflagrations that are also driven by climate forces, political calculations, and new subdivisions constructed in a drying out landscape. Dismantling these interlocking actions, and the systems they erected, is not simple. Not to do so is a choice that has deadly consequences.

The same can be said about the struggle to eliminate fossil fuels. *Unearthed* explores some of the dimensions of the enduring challenge to decarbonize the economy by tracking the past ten years of debate in California over hydraulic fracturing, or fracking. The Golden State is not the only political jurisdiction wrestling with this volatile issue—indeed, this chapter begins with my eavesdropping on a conversation with some of its technicians in northeastern Pennsylvania. And while the tactics that opponents developed in one state are often used in another, each locale's political culture and its contending voices are different enough that what happens in the West is not exactly what occurs in the East. Because California is the seventh largest producer of oil and gas in the nation, and its productive capacity generates a great deal of money for corporate entities and the state treasury, attempts to slow down, even shutter, this economic engine have been met with fierce resistance—from the governor, to the legislature, and in public opinion. Still, an intersectional coalition of environmental and social justice advocates has pursued innovative, bottom-up strategies.

Equally complex and earthbound are the ongoing efforts to reimagine water in California, the topic of *Watersheds*. Much of the re-conception begins with the definitive geological structure of a watershed. Its boundaries, from mountainous source through canyon mouth, follow streambeds as they weave across valley floor on their way to the ocean beyond. Not always visible, some waterways like the inland Mojave River are mostly subterranean, intermittent in flow, and disappear into a wash of sand, rock, and gravel. Even then, the watershed defined life within its reach, a reality that determined the locations of Indigenous communities and sustained their land management and ritual practices. However aware Euro-Americans may have been of the power of watersheds to frame human activities, their agricultural and later industrial economies led them to conclude water was a manipulable object that could be dammed, diverted, funneled, pumped, and flushed — and monetized. But there were often devastating consequences in these technological solutions.

That vital desert springs in the 1.6 million-acre Mojave Trails National Monument would be drained if another of these technological solutions was approved underscores the complex, landscape-scale impacts of human action. Effects that might outstrip the capacity of legislative efforts to protect imperiled place. This is one of the themes running through *Safe Havens*. Each essay addresses a national park, forest, monument, or marine sanctuary. Each area demonstrates that their national status as a protected place, as important and iconic as they may be, raises additional questions about the history of these environments and their contemporary dilemmas. Even the crown jewel of California parks, Yosemite, has its wild beauty bound up with the violent dispossession of its original and Indigenous inhabitants. Los Padres National Forest, along the state's central coast, equally implicated in the suppression of Indigenous Peoples, suffers from modern day trespassers growing an illegal crop. Other essays explore the protections and problems of safe havens—from one in a desert in Nevada to another in the Pacific so vast it would be the second largest state in the US.

On a different scale, sustaining community is a localized impulse that frames the final chapter, *Niche,* about Claremont, California where I live and work. The storylines often bloom during one stroll or another. Walking into the local branch of the county library system and noticing some of its exhibits led to a better understanding of the town's late nineteenth century founding. A memory of a day in 1973 spent clearing brush in Palmer Canyon sparked a reflection on the community's vulnerability to wildfires. A scientific paper on freeway-generated air pollution meant I should chart a different set of morning constitutionals, and rambling along sidewalks instructed me in how the city was put together over time. Other essays focus on those elements that might encourage and enhance Claremont's sustainability—green building codes, greater density, and a deliberate commitment to a more just and inclusive community. A set of responsibilities that can and should be dug into the landscape, a repatriation of this locale's once-indigenous plant-habitats, remnants of which can be seen in the foothills and the local botanic garden.

At an even smaller scale, there's our backyard. Despite the deed from the Los Angeles County Registrar-Recorder which stipulates this is our property, a garrulous mockingbird suggests otherwise, as would the Cooper's hawk that occasionally commandeers the telephone pole rising above the southeast corner of our lot. Coyotes testify that our land is on loan. Most mornings, I walk with these sure-footed mammals—whether I spot them or not. Invariably it's a single animal, rangy and furtive, hunting. It was unusual, then, to see a pair slip out of a vacant lot, turn north up Mountain Avenue, then veer down our street. Ten minutes later I arrived home to a story. My wife had gone to the back to fill the bird bath and when she looked up from the spigot, she startled what I suspect was one of the coyotes. It had cornered a stray cat against our fence, but the instant the hunter glanced at my wife, its intended prey clawed up the wooden slats to safety. Breakfast deferred, the coyote turned and ambled out along the driveway. Curious, I retraced its chase into the sage-scented garden, dropped to my knees and there, amid the oak-leaf litter, pressed into the dew-wet soil, a perfect pawprint.

RE/CREATION

Walking Through a Pandemic

I walk. A lot. I always have but now with an unsettled drive. Restless.

Being confined by the Covid-19 lockdown has ironically increased the miles I clock. Pandemic prohibitions have closed public parks in my hometown of Claremont, a college community on the eastern edge of Los Angeles County, bounded on the north by the San Gabriel Mountains and enveloping valley suburbs in every other direction. I miss my morning treks up into the dry, shrubby chaparral-studded foothills or along dusty Thompson Creek Trail, which demarcates hill from dale. Instead, I have been hugging closer to interior neighborhoods, at dawn, high noon, or dusk, whether dry or wet.

Not too far from my house is the Bernard Field Station, nearly ninety acres of protected coastal sage habitat. Walking its chain-link perimeter, I follow a chattering convoy of lesser goldfinch. They scatter as I breeze past, flitting through the diamond-shaped openings in the fence. The imposing structure is designed to keep us out: Private Property, the signs read. For these avian acrobats, it's portal and playground and perch.

A mile or so south, day breaks at a Metrolink commuter-train crossing: my eyes are struck not by the sun as it rises above snow-wreathed Mount San Gorgornio well to the east, but by the first rays as they slide along the curving steel rails turning them gold. Solar alchemy.

At walk's end, a pair of blue-flecked western fence lizards stretched out on our driveway, luxuriating in the morning's warmth. The second my sneaker touches down, they dart under thick mounds of shrubby baccharis, purple-flowered showy penstemon, or mounded buckwheat—indigenous plants we dug into the alluvial soil for our pleasure but which the lizards have turned into habitat, home.

Crimped by where I can wander, I've found myself listening more carefully, looking more closely, and smelling more discriminatingly. On rainy mornings with bandana on, glasses fogged—we've enjoyed many during the spring of 2020—I map my path to brush by the California Botanical Garden and its heaven-scent coastal sage biota. Transporting.

From there, I veer north along rain-splatted asphalt, leaping over dimpled puddles toward the nearest gash in the landscape: a hard-edged, straight-walled flood-control channel. The ripple, wash, and sluice of water bring a musical clatter of pebbles.

That noon, the skies clear, the heat spikes, and steam drifts from dark bark and grey shingle. The thin, razor-thin yucca, silhouetted against a pitted concrete-block wall, offers a stiff shadow. Pushing east, my slipstream rustles a cotton-candy lantana, and startlingly the bush seems to rise upward, until, Escher-like, it dissolves into a kaleidoscope of painted ladies; one of the butterflies lands on my brim, its wings pulsing. Still.

After lift-off its jittery dance disappears into the brightening day. I'm distracted by another set of aerial maneuvers wheeling above a friend's mid-century ranch. Slowly gaining elevation via a kettle of warm air, ten, maybe a dozen, no seventeen turkey vultures lazily wheel. As they feel the lip of its apex, one by one their feathered black wings tilt and glide away to the south.

By then I'm at the rounded corner where two streets intersect. Scrawled in rainbow-hued chalk, smudged but legible, the words of poet Ross Gay bend with the sidewalk like the graceful curve of apian wings: "thank you to the bee's shadow, perusing these words as I write them."

This beguiling, humbling vision begs another. But first, look up. A rare admonition, because in Southern California, as elsewhere, the sky view has been clouded by the toxic emissions we daily have pumped into the air from tailpipes and smokestacks. Now, with cars parked, and trains, planes, and trucks idled, the sky is dazzling. By day, it's azure. By night, it's so ebony that my evening stroll is more of a stumble as I try to put one foot in front of the other while craning my neck to pan the star-lit universe, anchored by a waxing moon and Venus bright.

Somewhere to my west, perhaps roosting in the upper story of the sentinel-like pine at the end of the block, a pair of great horned owls call. Grounded.

Rising Tides

Come summer, our son and daughter, Ben and Rebecca, and I built sandcastles by the sea. Make that "seas," for we scooped with our buckets and dug with our shovels along the three coasts that give shape to the nation's boundaries. But although the waters' names changed, and the size, shape, and complexity of our structures varied, the larger point of this annual exercise remained the same: hold back the tide.

A futile gesture, to be sure, as the legendary King Canute recognized when he reportedly sought to extend his dominion beyond the highwater mark. We were continually dismayed, too, when the pounding surf ignored our unstated command, first undercutting then flattening our fortifications. Thinking back on it now, I realize I missed the existential current that swirled beneath our pilgrimage to the ocean: death.

Its pull was always there. Standing in the roiling undertow, feeling the rocks rattle against my ankles, kelp wrapping around my calves, while the sand was sucked from beneath my feet, being knocked over by a rising wave as easily as its onward rush drowns yet another sandcastle. How could I miss those moments as metaphors?

Really, it wasn't that hard. I've lived on beaches for much of my life, at least for most of my childhood and adolescence, and consequently have lived *for* them ever since. They're a tantalizing middle ground, a zone between land and water in which life teemed, a place of re/creation. Procreation, too, I happily learned when, at twelve, I spied a couple copulate behind a dune; a stirring moment that with the onset of puberty I yearned to replicate. No such luck. Still, is it any wonder that sand is a sign of youthful promise?

Its premise is more complicated, of course; the strand has always been littered with clues about death and decay. The signs are as subtle as cracked mollusk shells tangled in matted clumps of seaweed left high and dry by the falling tide and as blunt as the massive rotting carcass of a sea lion that lay half-buried on a northern California beach. The baked mammal's pungent odor, the physical nearness of its death, had spooked Rebecca, but the next year, when she stumbled upon a dead harbor seal, she was unfazed.

"It's fate," she mused.

I better understood her point when our neighbor died. We had not been particularly close with Duff, though we lived within a hundred yards of one another. For one thing, his lawn was immaculate, ours reflected a decade of neglect. He was a native son and we were transplants, our politics rooted in different traditions. We regularly canceled out one another's vote. But these distinctions evaporated when, at only forty-two, he died, a death that struck home in part because of his home.

That's where his Rosary service was performed, its quiet, mantra-like chant—"Hail Mary, full of Grace..."—swelling throughout his house. My eyes wandered over its various rooms, each one of which bore his impress: he had hammered down every nail, molding, and floorboard. He modernized the kitchen, designed and built the rough-hewn family room, and added a bathroom, with copper ceiling and cedar walls. Over the years he had erected this mass, reordering its space to give precise architectural shape to his family's life. This man's home was his castle.

Its sturdy walls, however, could not hold off the cancer cells that bore from within, an erosive force that tore down his once-powerful frame, draining his fierce will to live. Duff was an old man at midlife whose skin, I thought when I last saw him, was the color of wet sand.

That damp grayness was everywhere underfoot as I walked along the Santa Barbara coast a few months later, forcing me to sift through my emotional attachment to beaches. It made me rethink the meaning of that city's many seawalls, thrown up to repulse the surging energy of the northern Pacific and shore up collapsing waterfront property. Long stretches have been undermined, leaving jagged slabs of concrete embedded in the beach, like toppled tombstones drifting out toward the ocean. In their wake were left badly eroded and scarred bluffs, the very thing the walls had been designed to prevent.

It won't be long before the remaining bulwarks come tumbling down, too, I thought. Many were deeply pitted from the rocks and debris hurled against them during heavy winter storms. A relentless sea was reclaiming its own, returning concrete to its constituent elements. Ashes to ashes, dust to dust.

Others have had similar grave thoughts, as the graffiti sprayed across these walls, broken and smooth-faced, reflected. It bore no resemblance to the territorial markings of urban gangs, but the spray-painted inscriptions spoke to another instinct of the human condition:

"We Luv You: Will Moller, RIP"
"Jhon Chiaig, Friend to All"
"Manuel Hyde, 64-92, RIP"

Occasionally, the mourners return to touch up these bids for immortality, imprints that faded in the wash of salt spray and sunlight. To do so required that they climb over another sign, this one in red block print: Danger: Unstable Wall. Its evocative warning no more restrained these eulogists than it did my children and I when a crashing wave battered our latest castle and we hastily slung buckets of sand into the breach.

Recreating the San Gabriels

Mount Wilson isn't the tallest peak in the San Gabriel Mountains — the craggy range that serves as the spine of the Angeles National Forest. Framing the northern backdrop to metropolitan Los Angeles, the San Gabriels annually lure millions of visitors to its boulder-strewn creeks, rugged trails, and windswept peaks. But for early twentieth-century humorist Mina Deane Halsey, Mount Wilson was plenty high enough. Reaching its 5,700-foot summit, she joked, was "the nearest station to Heaven yours truly ever expects to get."

That's because she prayed that she would never again have to ride a mule up the mountain's rocky, switchback trail, through rough-and-tumble terrain that decades earlier John Muir had dubbed "rigidly inaccessible." Halsey would come to share the great naturalist's wary insight. "The trip up Mt. Wilson makes me heave many sighs," she wrote. "In fact, I heaved so many sighs for weeks after that trip, that I had a hard time making anyone believe I had a good time. But I did."

Likely she had a difficult time recollecting Mount Wilson's joys due to an unnamed burro. "It takes four — five — six or seven hours to get up the trail, and it only took *me* somewhere around forty minutes to come down. Of course, most people don't hurry so on the down trip, but some things are forced upon us in this world, and that jackass of mine certainly knew his business." The many jolts and bruises notwithstanding, and despite the self-deprecating jokes she wrung from them, Halsey conceded there "were some wonderful sights along the way," including a glorious sunset at the trail's end.

That she made the trek at all is a testament to the power of outdoor recreation in local culture. High-country tourism in Southern California got its start in the 1880s, as Los Angeles's population boomed, and record-breaking numbers of snowbirds boarded trains in Chicago, Baltimore, or New York to experience the region's balmy, sun-kissed winter. Apparently, they were not put off by John Muir's haunting image of the local mountains: "The whole range, seen from the plain, with the hot sun beating upon its southern slopes, wears a terribly forbidding aspect. From base to summit all seems gray, barren, silent — dead, bleached bones of mountains."

Instead, they hit the trail, as had Halsey, following the paths that the Tongva and other Indigenous Peoples first blazed centuries earlier, and which was later widened to accommodate two-way traffic. Other routes were newly cut through chaparral-choked canyons and crested many of the more accessible mountains. To reach the stables, hotels, lodges, restaurants, and campgrounds constructed along these routes, nature seekers rode the Pacific Electric streetcar directly to the trailhead. This rail-to-trail infrastructure sustained and stimulated what would be called the region's "Great Hiking Era."

Much of this development preceded the December 1892 creation of the San Gabriel Timberland Reserve, the first such protected area to be established in California, and later renamed the Angeles National Forest. Given its recreational lure and legacy, it's surprising that the energetic bustle of tourists, hikers, hoteliers, and outfitters did not figure more often in the petitions seeking the initial reserve status. Those urging the Department of the Interior, which at that time managed these public lands, to create a reserve instead pushed for federal regulation of its most critical resource—water.

Forest advocate and real estate developer Abbot Kinney was among the first to urge the protection of these mountain watersheds. "Native growths of brush and chaparral, scrub oak, greasewood, sagebrush" increasingly were being "removed from the land by clearing and fire," he wrote in 1880, adding that all the "mesas are bare of verdure." These environmental alterations left downstream communities and agriculture more vulnerable to winter flooding and summer drought. Kinney concluded in an 1886 report from the State Board of Forestry, on which he served, that "the destruction of the forests in the southern counties means the destruction of the streams, and that means the destruction of the country."

Six years later, prominent citizens, grassroots organizers, irrigation districts, and chambers of commerce, as well as local congressional representatives, successfully appealed to Interior Secretary John W. Noble to address this problem. The secretary submitted to President Benjamin Harrison a proclamation creating the San Gabriel Reserve. It became one of fifteen reserves Harrison established using the Forest Reserve Act of 1891 that had granted the chief executive authority to designate "public reservations."

The president set the stage for a radical new conception of the purposes of the public domain, those federal lands the government owned in the western states and territories.

Previously, Congress's ambition had been to sell or give away these many millions of acres to homesteaders, farmers, loggers, and miners—not to say railroad corporations—to encourage settlement and development. By the late nineteenth century, this policy had gained an array of detractors. Communities worried about the rapid depletion of local forests and grasslands found common cause with conservationists and scientists concerned that damaged environments could not be regenerated. The loss of a landscape appealing to tourists as well as the loss of critical water sources would devastate the economy.

These and other engaged citizens advocated for a more robust nation-state to intercede to protect the public lands and the resources they contained. A petition submitted in favor of the San Gabriel Reserve asserted the government's protective presence would ensure that "the water would be preserved in the mountains, the snow saved from being speedily melted, the waters protected from pollution by large droves of cattle and sheep."

The notion that managing nature upstream to sustain human interests downstream, and that Washington could and should resolve local disputes over resource allocation and consumption, signaled a broader desire for a more efficient and effective federal government. The call for making public life more orderly, rational, and manageable was a hallmark of Progressive Era reform and activism and created what some historians call the Administrative State. Emblematic of this era's ethos was the establishment of the initial forest reserves, as well as the later formation of the Forest Service to manage them.

The San Gabriel Mountains revealed how fire could complicate this benign scenario. The range's topography and ecology have conspired against the human desire to exclude fire from this landscape. Muir, during a three-day hike in 1875, recorded some of the features that have frustrated firefighters ever since: sheer-walled canyons, treacherously loose soils, and ridges "weathered away to a slender knife-edge," the whole thickly covered in a "bristly mane of chaparral."

This terrain comes alive when it erupts in flame. At lower elevations, the dominant plant community is the fire-adapted chaparral. It provides a combustible fuel that if ignited on days of high wind, low humidity, and intense heat can create firestorms of immense and swirling power. Not everyone who has lived within the Los Angeles Basin has seen these flames as detrimental to their way of life. Indigenous People used fire to manage hillside ecosystems to produce more highly prized plants and animals. The Spanish did the same to promote grasslands for their livestock. These two groups knew enough not to live within the fire zones — the foothills, notched canyons, and upland slopes. Not so for late nineteenth-century outdoor enthusiasts and those seeking domestic solitude from the burgeoning city below. For these newcomers, fire became a problem that must be solved.

Their concerns were captured in newspaper accounts of the frequent conflagrations. In 1878, as fire roared through the foothills above Pasadena, the *San Francisco Chronicle* reported that "5 canyons were desolated ... [and a] tongue of flames could be seen licking its way up the San Gabriel range of mountains," a destructive image the *Los Angeles Times* replicated whenever the local skies turned black with smoke. "Ten-Mile Wall of Flame Rushing on Ridge Route," one headline screamed; another mourned, "Canyon Fire Rages Unchecked."

Public outcry turned political, generating demands for more robust firefighting forces at the local, state, and federal levels. Later, two governmental agencies would spend much of their tiny budgets each summer and fall trying to stamp out fire. One was the Forest Service, which managed the Angeles National Forest after its creation in 1905, and the other was the Los Angeles County Board of Forestry, which was founded in 1911 and oversaw one million acres of adjacent lands.

There was another, more effective way of managing these conflagrations, the Mission Indian Federation wrote President Calvin Coolidge after a series of devastating fires in the mid-1920s. Return these lands to the Indigenous People, who for millennia had managed these flammable landscapes *with* fire. The president demurred. A century later, intense firefighting continues to consume the county's and the Forest Service's time and money. "The story of ranger activity in the Angeles National Forest," one local historian commented, "is a story primarily of fire control."

That is still true, but contemporary fire suppression comes with even greater pressure: millions of people now live very close to the national forest, making their protection job number one. Notwithstanding the advent of innovative firefighting tools such as flame-retardant-dropping aircraft, controlling fire remains as partial a solution as it was years ago. By their very nature, these lands burn.

Yet for all the Angeles's dangers, which escalate whenever post-fire, debris-filled floods churn down the ravines and scour everything in their path, millions of people take advantage of this jagged landscape's recreational opportunities. Perhaps like Halsey, they too test themselves against its daunting wildness, and, laughing, tell stories about how they have come up short.

Trail Mix

I mean this in the nicest possible way—take a hike!

Don a pair of sturdy shoes, boots, even tennies. Slip on a hat, slap on some suntan lotion, and bring water in a reusable bottle. Then head to the nearest urban park, wildlife refuge, or forested trailhead. Once there, start walking.

If you put heel-to-toe on the first Saturday in June, you'll be celebrating National Trails Day. The fact that there is such a designation tells us something about how sedentary American life has become. The American Hiking Society established this day-outing in 1993 to build public interest in and support for the more than 200,000 miles of trails that crisscross the United States, from fruited plain to purple mountain majesties, and everything between, however rough or gentle the grade.

The amazing number of trail miles is almost five times the miles devoted to the interstate highway system. Let's face it, hiking—even if we are puffing along, or red-of-cheek—is a lot better for us than revving up the Chevy and putting it on cruise control. So says the AHS: "Trails provide opportunities to breathe fresh air, get hearts pumping, escape from daily stresses and maintain overall health."

While salubrious, heading out also can be liberating. Henry David Thoreau, that inveterate walker, certainly thought so. He spilled a lot of ink chalking up the virtues of trekking, or as he would have it, sauntering. This latter word's derivation had several sources, he affirmed, one of which was from the French, sans terre: "without land or a home. Which, therefore…will mean, having no particular home, but equally at home everywhere."

Especially places where humans lived not. Thoreau opens his canonical essay, "Walking," with these words: "I wish to speak a word for Nature, for absolute freedom and wildness," because he wanted to make it clear that he "regarded man as an inhabitant, or a part and parcel of Nature, rather than a member of society." To accept that claim required another, the belief that "in Wildness is the preservation of the World."

What does this mean? Bumper-sticker ideologues often reverse wilderness preservation's intent, arguing that it's required to create landscapes in which humans have no place; the wild is devoid of people, a conception that justified the creation of national parks and forests that in turn legitimized the erasure of the Indigenous presence in the land. That was not what Thoreau had in mind: rather, he was talking about the human experience of nature, our mediation about it as we saunter through it.

His journeys were usually pretty pedestrian: "our expeditions are but tours," he admitted, "and come round again at evening to the old hearthside from which we set out." Yet in the time it took to circle back, his consciousness of place correspondingly would shift. To trek was to become mindful. To walk was to think.

You don't have to adopt Thoreau's transcendental vision to enjoy these unfettered moments outdoors, even in the most urban of settings (as mine often are). There is, after all, something riveting about watching a great white egret standing stock-still in the swirling waters of the Los Angeles River's Glendale Narrows, cars and trucks whizzing overhead on the Golden State Freeway; and then watch it strike, a flash of silver in its yellow bill.

Every bit as startling was the moment when my wife and I rounded a bend in the marshlands of the upper reach of Newport Bay, and caught this strange drama: on an exposed tree limb, an osprey, also called a sea hawk and whose diet is heavily fish-dependent, was dining on a squirrel. Nature provides.

That's part of the wilderness. But also listen to the clatter of rock and shell as Pacific rollers sweep ashore at Will Rogers State Beach. Peer down into the thin flow of Salt Creek in Death Valley, hoping to glimpse that Ice-Age relict, the minuscule pup fish. On a baking August afternoon, high up in the Santa Anas, catch a random whiff of sage. Nature abides.

To be at home in these disparate places requires us to enter them. That obligation is in part what drives my students and colleagues up into the hills, out across the desert, from tidal pool to coastal bluff, grassland to arroyo, sidewalk to greensward.

Richard Ross, a friend and colleague, doesn't hesitate to name his favorite hike: the Puente Hills, a mere twenty miles from downtown Los Angeles. This low chain of hills, part of the region's transverse ranges, contains remnants of chaparral and oak woodlands ecosystems, set within native grasses. Of special note are the Turnbull Canyon trails, Richard declares, which rise out of the city of Whittier's streetscape, a relatively easy climb set within an increasingly dry and rugged terrain. Once you reach the ridgeline, a thousand feet above the valley floor, the Pacific glitters to the south and west, downtown Los Angeles mirrors back the sun, and if you pivot east the San Gabriels soar above. This walk, he advises, "is a great blend, in a Thoreauvian sense, of the domesticated and the wild: not too wild, but not too tame either."

As devoted to Southland hiking is Wayne Steinmetz, a retired colleague whose enthusiasm for the San Gabriels is unmatched. Fast of foot, he is every bit as speedy in ticking off a series of mountainous landmarks — the classic "Bridge to Nowhere" trail along the east fork of the San Gabriel River and Mount Baden Powell with its killer views of the San Andreas Rift zone. The best view of all, though, was well west, up to Mount San Jacinto, which at 10,834-feet dominates the eponymous mountains in Riverside County. Despite its height, he swears its ascent "is not a death march." Good call.

Worth the climb Wayne assures because the summit offers the best views in all Southern California — from the pan-hot desert to the icy peaks of the San Gorgonio Wilderness. John Muir agreed, enthusing the mountain was the "most sublime spectacle to be found anywhere on this earth!"

Muir liked exclamation points and similarly enthused about his beloved Sierras. So does Ross Brennan, one of my former students. It helps to know that he grew up in the Sierra, has spent summers living in a tent above treeline in the Rockies conducting biological research, and that his peers lovingly dubbed him the "Mountain Man," his wild hair and beard befitting the nickname. While an undergraduate in Claremont, Ross spent his four years exploring jagged upcountry. His favorite terrain was the Cucamonga Wilderness Area. It received congressional protection in 1964, in the first year of the Wilderness Act, a 12,781-acre swath studded with Douglas fir, and Jeffrey and

Ponderosa pine, an arboreal shelter for mountain lions, bears, and Nelson bighorn sheep. This biodiversity appealed to the ecologist in Ross, but what really struck him was a certain familiarity. "What I like about these high elevation hikes of the San Gabriels is that their mountainous environs feel so different than much of what 'Southern California' embodies. They are cold, have beautiful old pines, a splashing stream, and they're steep. You can even see the stars at night. Maybe I just feel at home."

Another whose footing seems most secure on precarious ground is a keen-sighted geologist, the indefatigable Rick Hazlett. His legendary field trips to estuaries, salt flats, and sand dunes, like his mountain tramps, are done at quick time, perhaps no surprise as he is the son of a decorated Marine test-pilot. That you need endurance to keep up with him is clear from his description about why he leaps at the chance to clamber up Strawberry Peak in the San Bernadino Mountains with its "beautiful conifer forest and aerobic climb."

To slow him down, Rick's students stall: "what's this tree?" (pant, pant). "Remind me the name of that upthrust" (gasp). "This ... is ... a ... refugium?" No fool, the dedicated teacher answers as he keeps moving, firing back with his own questions — covering all things geological, hydrological, and ecological. The trail is just another classroom.

Anna Kramer is among those who got schooled. Her initial response to the Claremont Hills Wilderness Park, a five-mile loop through the local foothills, was that it was "too representative of all the things I was struggling to adjust to in LA: the crowds, the heat, the incessant sun, the crowds, needing to drive to the trailhead, the crowds ... did I say the crowds?" Over time, however, she became acclimated, so much so that "the other people (and dogs, of course) on the trail became the reason that the CHWP loop became my favorite." In this automobile-centric region, here was a respite from the car—people walked, ran, and biked. "And jogged with their weighted vests and pumped uphill with their hand weights. And chatted with family and friends as they caught their breath under the scrub oaks and at the summits." The diversity of people with whom she shared the trails, the manifold languages they spoke, "helped me start to unravel the particular normative ideals I held about what being 'outdoorsy' entailed."

To hike can shift one's point of view. Other friends recount that whenever they are feeling muffled beneath the thick, cool, gray marine layer of early summer, they lace up and start climbing. Soon enough they break through May gray or June gloom, Southern California's morning marine layer, into the brilliant summer sky. What you feel depends on where you stand.

What you see depends on what you understand. So affirmed Mary Austin, whose brilliant memoir, *The Land of Little Rain* (1903), contains luminous insights about her life in the Eastern Sierra and the workings of the high desert, the Mojave. She listened to its ancient people speak of this land without borders; struck up conversations with a Pocket Hunter, a prospector, who had "that faculty of small hunted things of taking on the protective color of his surroundings."

But it was from those small hunted things themselves that she learned the most essential facts. Getting down on her hands and knees, getting down "to the eye level of rat and squirrel kind," Austin wrote, was the only way she could perceive the "slender threads of barrenness" that guided these furry creatures great and small to spring or sink, to any moisture: "Venture to look for some seldom-touched water-hole, and so long as the trails run with your general direction make sure you are right, but if they begin to cross yours at never so slight an angle, to converge toward a point left of right of your objective, no matter what the maps say, or your memory, trust them; they know."

Her emphatic affirmation, and the canny perception that underlies it, can only be acquired by spending time, lots of time, out-of-doors.

Take a hike.

Flower Power

The admonition is instructive: Leave No Trace. That this three-word imperative is capitalized, only reinforces the idea that They Really Mean It. Which begs the question: Who are They, and what do they Mean?

Before backtracking through the history of Leave No Trace, here is a recent example of the human behavior in the wild it seeks to curb.

The time: Spring 2017

The scene: the 640,000-acre Anza-Borrego Desert State Park, the biggest in California's system and the nation's second largest behind New York's Adirondack State Park

The setting: a vast physical space, two-thirds the size of Rhode Island, in desert-badlands-and-mountainous terrain as arid, hot, and rugged as anywhere on the planet

The expectation: the human imprint at Anza-Borrego would be relatively minimal. You can disappear here. So will your footprints, swept away by the dust-filled wind. The only eternal thing is the place itself.

The conundrum: what is arguably this desert's most ephemeral living thing—wildflowers—may generate the most anthropogenic damage

The explanation: #Superbloom2017

"It's a madhouse."

I'm not sure which one of us blurted out those words, but as my wife Judi and I drove into Anza-Borrego on a Thursday morning in the first week of that March, we encountered hundreds of cars lining up to squeeze into a jammed lot at park headquarters. Other drivers, frustrated by the wait, simply pulled off the road wherever they found space, their vehicles canted like so many pick-up-sticks scattered across a floor. Trying to control the gridlock, a lone ranger, frantic and arm-waving, wasn't having much luck.

In search of an off-site information kiosk, we inched past the gridlock and headed for a nearby strip mall; the crowd surrounding the Anza-Borrego Foundation trailer was thick in number and querulous in voice. We all thought we'd beat the crowd by visiting midweek. Within minutes of our collective arrival, we learned that the only thing more numerous than the extraordinary profusion of wildflowers was the human swarm descending, like locusts, on fields of orange, purple, white, yellow, and green.

I felt my complicity every step of the way, even after we got out of the way, as far away as possible, heading by down rutted dirt roads that winter floods had turned into washboards. Those waters were the reason why sand verbena, desert lilies and dandelions, and arroyo lupines stretched out as far as the eye could see, a multi-hued carpet rolling right up to the dark sandstone mountains that framed the valley floor. We walked lightly, or as lightly as we could under the circumstances: tip-toeing through the natural bouquets, avoiding the densest arrangements, and even trying hard not to break the sunbaked mud, its shards creating a quilt-like, geometric structure that anchored the yellow-flecked creosote bushes above.

An impossible commitment, Leave No Trace. The pressure of a single pair of boots will leave an impression. Add tens of thousands of toes and heels, and regardless of whether the outsoles are soft or hard, flat or textured, no matter the care taken, the landscape will be pounded. A churned aftermath of bent stems, flattened petals, uprooted plants.

Even snapping a photograph can leave an indelible imprint. Many hustled to Anza-Borrego after flicking through captivating, online images of the superbloom, intensifying the crush. Some were disappointed when the virtual appeared more beguiling than the real. One crew of friends lured to the park by what they expected to encounter, came away unimpressed.

"I was hoping to see purple waves," a young woman told the *Los Angeles Times*. "Not dots of yellow."

Her companion concurred: "This isn't what it looked like on social media."

Long before Pinterest, Facebook, or Instagram, the Great Outdoors drew people in. The numbers racing to embrace Mother Earth in the decades immediately following World War II were staggering. Thirty-three million visited the national forests in 1950; twenty years later more than 172 million hit the trails. Deeply worried about the wear and tear on the 193 million acres it stewarded, the US Forest Service developed an outdoor-education program called No Trace. Its original principles included teaching visitors how to practice low-impact hiking and camping, be sensitive to the needs of other species and the habitats that sustain them, and respect what makes wilderness wild.

Other federal and state agencies, whose lands were as buffeted, joined with the Forest Service to expand these concepts and develop educational materials to extend their reach. In 1990, the Forest Service contracted with the National Outdoor Leadership School (NOLS) to create low-impact pedagogy and training. From this work emerged Leave No Trace and its seven-step program:

- Plan Ahead and Prepare
- Travel and Camp on Durable Surfaces
- Dispose of Waste Properly
- Leave What You Find
- Minimize Campfire Impacts
- Respect Wildlife
- Be Considerate of Other Visitors

Anza-Borrego State Park was an early adopter of these concepts, reframed appropriately as Desert Ethics. Its brochures aimed at hikers, campers, cyclists, and day-trippers come stamped in boldface with another 1960s-derived mantra: Leave only footprints. Take only memories. The message is essential, yet its commandment-like imperative, cannot impel people to regulate themselves. Particularly when they see others plopping down on one clump of daisies to take photos of another cluster.

I'm not complaining about rude rubes, those who love nature to death without much thought, rather I'm suggesting our outdoor-educational aspirations may miss a larger point. Leave No Trace assumes that built and natural landscapes are so distinct that they require different modes of behavior. Yet what if this perceived binary—nature and civilization—is partly responsible for the very consequences park rangers want to temper? Perhaps it is time to launch an educational initiative that will teach us how to value and respect our urban environments—where most of us live, after all—with the same love we are urged to feel for the bucolic. Build more parks and dedicated open spaces. Plant more indigenous trees, bushes, and grasses. Rewild now-concretized rivers and streams. Think of our homes as habitats.

Doing so just might enable us to take better care of our local environs and those more distant, whether desert, mountainous, or coastal.

EMBERS

San Francisco

·Sacramento

Sierras

Santa
Barbara

·Los Angeles

·San Diego

1. North Complex/Bear
2. Mountain View
3. Eskirine
4. Thomas
5. Rye
6. Saddle Ridge
7. Skirball
8. Creek
9. La Tuna
10. Santiago
11. Bobcat
12. Blue Cut

Time to Pivot

Wildland fires are messy. They disrupt and transform ecosystems, threaten our home grounds, and their soot-filled skies, blackened terrain, and damaged watersheds have long-term, public-health ramifications.

Such conflagrations also incinerate the very language we employ when we try to describe them. The Rocky Fire of 2015, which consumed nearly 70,000 acres, an area equivalent to over eighty Central Parks, in Colusa, Lake, and Yolo counties in northern California, stunned veteran firefighters. Its intensity, erratic movements, and drought-fueled energy left them nearly speechless. As Jason Shanley, a Cal Fire spokesperson, understated: "This fire wants to do whatever it wants. It's defying all odds. Thirty-year, forty-year veterans have never seen this before."

Frontline firefighters were just as baffled by the nearby and hyper-explosive Jerusalem fire that erupted that August. A local marijuana farmer allegedly ignited it via an illegal backfire designed to protect his crop, but it escaped with a rush and in less than forty-eight hours raced through 12,000 parched acres. Had it merged with the larger Rocky Fire, it would have created a wind-whipped holocaust that would have outrun our capacity to speak of its significance.

As startling these dangerous fires appear, as amazed as we were at their fiery runs, they aren't unique. The 1889 Santiago fire in San Diego County incinerated more than 300,000 acres, according to contemporaries who watched in awe-struck silence. "Nothing like it occurred in California since the National Forests have been administered," forester L.A. Barrett acknowledged. "In fact, in my thirty-three years in the Service I have never seen a forest or brush fire to equal it."

Although not as large, early twentieth-century fires in the San Gabriel Mountains still shocked firefighters by their zig-zagging speed and the self-generated micro-climates such as powerful downdrafts and windstorms that disrupted efforts to suppress them. Later still, the mega-fire seasons of 2003 and 2007, along with the Station Fire of 2009 and the Rim Fire of 2013, blew past observers' estimates of their projected ferocity. Every generation has believed that its experience with wildland fires has been unprecedented.

Each generation has also placed its faith in a variety of technological fixes to solve the "problem" of fire. The founders of the national forest system, dating back to 1891, declared fires the enemy and asserted that with enough human and fiscal resources they could snuff them out. Their aspirations, never fully realized, were rebooted after World War II as firefighting agencies deployed surplus airplanes and bulldozers to attack fires large and small. These goals have been reengaged with the more recent use of satellite imagery, fire retardants, and drones as part of the firefighting arsenal.

Yet nature has routinely and continuously confounded our high-tech ambitions to control it.

That being the case, and in this age of climate disruption and deepening drought in the West, it's time to develop a more resilient approach to wildland-fire management. We must increase the funding at all levels to build more defensible and fire-safe landscapes around homes and communities; adding or expanding a minimal tax on those living in historic high-severity fire zones to pay for ongoing fire-safety education; and boosting firefighting budgets such that local, state, and federal agencies can spend other dollars on proactive, fire-preventative initiatives that might in advance minimize the growth of runaway flames.

There's nothing new about these steps, though the urgency for their application is accelerating. Firefighters will tell you that fire management requires managing people — especially those rooted into canyons, foothills, and ridgelines. Their growing presence in these beguiling landscapes have created lovely residences that serve as more fuel for fires to consume and more structures for firefighters to defend. Their high-dollar presence increases dangers for those who inhabit these sites of scenic view as they do for those who race uphill to protect them from fires like the Station, Rocky, and Jerusalem.

We must embrace the idea that large wildland fires are normal, that their very unpredictability is predictable, and that we need a comprehensible set of strategies to respond to the dangers they pose. The sooner we make this paradigm shift, the more likely we will find a way to coexist with their messy nature.

Fiery Past

The Erskine Fire in Kern County, California, which blew up in June 2016, was big, fast, and dangerous. Its power was evident in the tragic loss of life (an elderly couple, who could not escape in time) the incineration of an estimated one hundred and fifty structures and its rapid growth — more than 36,000 acres burned in its first thirty hours. Imagine an area the size of Staten Island in ashes.

Hundreds of firefighters on the ground and in the air struggled to get ahead of the inferno, while staying out of its fury. In the words of Kern County Fire Chief Brian Marshall: these men and women "have been engaged in a firefight of epic proportions trying to save every structure possible."

The Erskine Fire, which was the state's second largest that year, was frightening, too. "We've had lots of big incidents," said Captain Mike Nicholas of the Kern County force. "This one's pretty bad though." But as bad as the Erskine was, it wasn't unprecedented.

Indeed, its high-intensity flames, breakneck speed and erratic behavior were perfectly consistent with how large fires have always behaved in the southern Sierras. It's a rough landscape, particularly in the area framing the lower Kern Plateau that slopes down into the Fremont Valley to the south and west toward the Central Valley. Above its narrow canyons and meadows, the ridgelines are studded with Jeffrey and lodgepole pine, with some red fir thrown in for good measure. At lower elevations these woodlands are intermixed with and then replaced by dense, almost impenetrable thickets of chaparral—a tangle of chamise, manzanita, sages, and low-growing oaks and buckeyes.

Ecologists know that high-intensity, mixed-severity fires have been the norm in this portion of the Sierra for millennia. Many of the landscape's key species—trees and shrubs—are fire-dependent or fire-adapted. Surprisingly, without fire, these forests would not exist.

George B. Sudworth of the U.S. Division of Forestry (forerunner of the U.S. Forest Service) encountered historic evidence of fire when at the turn of the twentieth century he inspected the southern Sierras. Everywhere he went, he found that ancient blazes big and small had left their mark in high-elevation pine forests and chaparral-cloaked foothills, in canyons and on ridgelines. Lightning strikes caused some of the fires, while others were millennia-long consequences of Indigenous Peoples' fire-management for cultural resources, food, and ritual materials.

The more recent scarring had a different source. Sudworth blamed shepherds, miners, loggers, and hunters for fires that in some cases had been intentionally set, others the result of pre-Smoky Bear carelessness. Each had different aims when they struck a match: shepherds to convert brush into grasslands, miners to expose potential mineral veins, loggers to incinerate branches and other detritus, and hunters to open the landscape for a clear shot. About the conflagrations that erupted, many of the region's torch-bearing white settlers apparently couldn't have cared less: "it was all public land," E.W. Maslin, a resident of Loomis, said in 1889, "and what is everybody's business is nobody's business."

That indifference was born out of the small population in the vast Kern County. In 1890 it was home to fewer than ten thousand people, the vast majority living in flatland towns. But by the 1940s, the county's population was over 135,000 with clusters sheltering in hill and mountain communities. Consider the response, then, to a blaze that ignited in June of 1942 during World War II outside the Sequoia National Forest. Fueled by high winds, low humidity and searing heat, it raced across 51,000 acres—mostly chaparral and grass.

The next month those same weather conditions were critical to the growth and spread of three additional fires. The Rancheria Fire consumed nearly 6,000 acres; the Fish Hatchery Fire took out more than 23,000 acres; and the aptly named Stormy Canyon Fire, which an arsonist touched off, burned upwards of 21,000 acres. Exhausted fire crews and anxious residents, though they may have been far from the front lines of the furious global conflict, suffered their own form of battle fatigue.

That month-long swarm of conflagrations was significant for two reasons, observed fire historian Robert Cermak in *Fire in the Forest: A History of Forest Fire Control on the National Forests of California* (2005). The 1942 fire season "proved to be the worst in the history of the Sequoia National Forest," and the climate-driven character of these explosive fires testified to the "controlling role that weather plays in fire control in the Golden State."

His insight remained true when, in 2016, the Erskine Fire swept across the baked-dry southern Sierra. Yet for all its ferocity, that fire is part of an enduring pattern that has made the Sierra, the Sierra.

Burning Eyes

You didn't need to be flying into Ontario International Airport in June 2016 to know that Southern California's fire season had begun. But the view from 10,000 feet offered a unique perspective on how wildfires impact the region.

Descending through Cajon Pass, my flight cut through a slipstream of smoke riding the strong westerly winds that sweep along the southern face of the San Gabriel Mountains. The connection between the Southland's prevailing air currents and topography means that any fire burning in the Angeles National Forest, which is draped over the San Gabriels, will extend far beyond its point of ignition and acreage burned.

That was true for the Reservoir and Fish fires that erupted on June 20 and consumed more than 6,000 acres (roughly twelve Disneylands). Those living within the basin that extends from the San Gabriel Valley fifty miles east to Riverside and San Bernardino could not miss the smoke and haze hanging overhead, the white ash twirling down, or an acrid burning in their throats.

This bitter aftertaste even penetrated the jet that brought me home the day those two fires ignited. As it made its final approach, wheels down, the plane's pressurized cabin filled with the stench of burnt wood. A flight attendant had to calm out-of-state passengers by assuring them they were not smelling engine failure but forest fires nearly 30 miles away.

Locals may have smiled knowingly at our seatmates' initial distress, but we are not any more discerning about another consistent aspect of fire season—how we talk, and argue, about wildland conflagrations.

For the U.S. Forest Service, Cal Fire and county firefighting agencies, these blazes seem to have a single cause: the density of what they call "fuel." More than eighty percent of the forests in the San Gabriel, San Bernardino and San Jacinto mountains are composed of chaparral: in this context, "fuel" consists of shrubs such as ceanothus, sage, chamise, manzanita and related species. It's an indigenous ecosystem that when healthy grows thick, forming an impenetrable, clothes-tearing habitat that naturalist John Muir once affectionately praised as "thornily savage."

Fire agencies have never shared Muir's admiration for the prickly chaparral. Since the early twentieth century, they've tried to get rid of it. Strategies included supplanting the endemic biota by converting it to grassland or other ecotypes. These attempts failed.

Yet chaparral's competitiveness has not stopped public lands managers who argue that this habitat poses an extreme fire danger, so much so that it must be cleared away by mechanical means and chemicals. Huge machines called masticators chew up acres at a time. Herbicides are then sprayed to keep it from re-sprouting. For those who finger chaparral as Southern California's fire problem, shredding and poisoning it within the wildland-urban interface and deep in backcountry are the only ways to save life, limb, and landscape.

Not so. Historical records indicate that chaparral wildfires can be large but are also infrequent. Other researchers argue that the invasive grasses that move in once chaparral has been ground down burn hotter and faster—hardly a prescription for less fire. Ecologists affirm that neither the age of the chaparral forest nor its density determines when these fires will erupt or how they burn. Rather, chaparral fires are weather-driven phenomena occurring with high heat, low humidity, deep drought, and high, offshore winds known locally as Santa Anas. These conditions were present for the fast-moving Fish and Reservoir fires. Four years later, one of the largest fires in Los Angeles County, the Bobcat Fire, powered by powerful winds and record-setting heat, not only re-burned some acreage that its predecessors had torched, but raced up and over the San Gabriels. It consumed more than 117,000 acres before reaching the Antelope Valley on the northern edge of the mountain range.

Fire, in short, is inevitable. That's the big picture, whether looking down from 10,000 feet or studying the complex fire history of Southern California. Yet the agencies speak of battling enemy fire, and the media offer eye-catching images of soot-stained firefighters and orange-red fire retardants raining down. Another image is captured in the haunting words an acquaintance uttered while peering through a window at the smoke-filled, orange-tinged sky: "It's like death outside."

This frenzied narration, however understandable, reinforces the idea that all fire is bad and must be suppressed. It seems to me that a more insightful narrative framework—and firefighting strategy—is to learn how to better coexist with fire.

Forest for the Trees

The trees are dying. The forests are not.

This subtle but absolutely crucial distinction was lost in all the angst in 2016 over the tree die-off in the Central Sierra, coastal ranges, and other forests of the Golden State. Players ranging from the U.S. Forest Service to Cal Fire to U.S. Senator Dianne Feinstein and other public officials ignored this key fact in their rush to do something, anything, about the dying trees.

Senator Feinstein, for one, wrote to U.S. Agriculture Secretary Tom Vilsack urging him to transfer the tidy sum of $38 million to the Forest Service so that it could immediately harvest thousands of red-needled pine and other dead trees in high hazard areas in the Sequoia, Sierra, and Stanislaus national forests. "After five years of historic drought," she argued, "which has led to the death of an estimated sixty-six million trees in California alone, my state and its people face a heightened and potentially catastrophic risk of wildfire this year and for years to come."

Her request was a drop in the bucket. The Forest Service estimated conservatively that $562 million would be needed to clear cut 3.7 million trees on its lands in the state. There was no way that the Obama administration would ask Congress for, or that that legislative body would provide, half-a-billion dollars for this work in a single state.

More importantly, the calculation that dead trees equal catastrophe could not have been more wrong.

Although the attention-getting and widely publicized figure of sixty-six million dead trees (or "snags") seems huge, the figure shrinks when set in its wider, arboreal context. Doug Bevington of Environment Now reported there are thirty-three million forested *acres* in the state, meaning that the recent pulse of tree mortality on average has increased the number of dead trees by a mere two snags per acre. "To put that number in perspective, forest animals that live in snags generally need at least four to eight snags per acre to provide sufficient habitat and some species require even more snags." California's forests, in short, suffer from a *deficit* of dead trees, not a surfeit.

Besides, dead trees are not dead. They are essential to the life chances of such cavity-nesting species as the endangered California spotted owl and the increasingly rare black-backed woodpecker. The same holds true for the rarely seen Pacific fisher, a forest-dweller related to the weasel whose diet in part consists of small mammals that take advantage of snag-ecosystems. A host of organisms feasts on dead trees upright or fallen, so what on the surface might seem like a ghost forest is a biodiversity hotspot, a teeming terrain.

While countless living things thrive off the "dead" trees, fire does not. This seems counterintuitive, which may account for the head-scratching, heated rhetoric that Senator Feinstein, Governor Jerry Brown, and firefighting agencies deployed to make their case that California was on the verge of burning up. In doing so, they did not know about or dismissed the findings of fire-ecology research demonstrating that snags do not burn with a greater intensity and that their presence does not accelerate the spread of fire. As scientists reported in the *Proceedings of the National Academy of Sciences* (2014): "Contrary to the expectation of increased wildfire activity in recently infested red-stage stands, we found no difference between observed area and expected area burned in red-stage or subsequent gray-stage stands during three peak years of wildfire activity, which account for 46% of area burned during the 2002–2013 period." Even the state's firefighter-in-chief, Cal Fire's Director Ken Pimlott, agreed with the "emerging body of science that has found dead trees don't significantly increase the likelihood of wildfires."

Don't get me wrong: there are legitimate reasons to log some snags located in portions of the wildland-urban interface to ensure public safety and protect vital infrastructure. But slicking off tens of thousands of trees willy-nilly—let alone the 3.7 million that were proposed for harvest in the national forests alone—cannot be defended in terms of science or policy, and is an unnecessary expenditure of funds.

But neither should it be defended as a kind of political logrolling by agencies and their allies spreading fear of imminent ecosystemic collapse averted only through a massive infusion of federal and state dollars which would prop up the collapsing timber and biomass industries. The latter turns board-feet into kilowatts, a process as inefficient and carbon dioxide-spewing as coal, accelerating the planet's warming. Not climate smart.

As an alternative, what if we tried taking nature seriously? Those who mourn the loss of the iconic, pine-scented sweep of green, for example, should remember that the "death" we perceive in California's forests presages their regeneration. John Muir, the troubadour of all things Sierra, wrote as much in 1878. After all, his field research led him to conclude that Sequoia's regrowth depended on natural disturbance. Erosion and floods, the "burrowing of wolf or squirrel," and the "fall of aged trees" cleared the way for successive generations to flourish. Even fire, "the great destroyer of Sequoia … furnishes bare virgin ground, one of the conditions essential for its growth from seed." Muir's penetrating insight was controversial in the late nineteenth century, but it shouldn't be today.

The trees are dying. The forests are not.

Bonfire Politics

The major fires in the summer and fall of 2017 burned across more than eight million acres, an area larger than nine US states. They destroyed an estimated $2 billion-worth of property and rained lung-clogging ash on residents in major cities such as Seattle, Portland, Los Angeles, and points east. These fires, like those in the preceding years, should have jolted policymakers into a full-on assessment of wildland fire, its climate drivers and forest-health consequences.

Alas, that was the last thing the then-Trump administration was interested in doing. Its key officials—Interior Secretary Ryan Zinke, Agriculture Secretary Sonny Perdue, and EPA Administrator Scott Pruitt—refused to acknowledge the primary role that dangerous climatological factors, such as drought, heat, and wind, have played in energizing and propelling wildland fire. Instead, while visiting Montana's Lolo Peak fire, they fingered "radical environmentalists" who allegedly scuttled timber sales that would have removed trees and reducing ignition sources.

How ironic that undercutting the Trump triumvirate's claims was that very 53,000-acre burn they used for dramatic backdrop to their press conference. The forests around Lolo Peak had been repeatedly logged in recent years and yet they still erupted in flame. The reason? "Large fires are not like campfires," Dominick DellaSala and Timothy Ingalsbee, two wildfire scientists, observed: "they are mainly driven by extreme weather conditions, not fuels."

This on-the-ground reality did not deter Secretary Zinke from ignoring fire science in a post-trip memo to Interior land management staff. "For our managers and superintendents of units that have burnable vegetation," Zinke wrote, "I am directing you to think about fire in a new and aggressive way." Getting aggressive consisted of solely of removing "the steady accumulation of fuels on our nation's public lands and the resulting increased threats from catastrophic wildfires." By reducing the value of trees and other woody vegetation to "fuel," Zinke could insist that logging alone would solve the threat of wildland fire—despite mounting evidence to the contrary.

His real intention was to gut the regulatory authorities of the National Environmental Policy Act (NEPA). Zinke and crew tipped their hand in Montana when they argued against the Act's requirement for rigorous environmental impact reports and its principles of public input and oversight. Their goal was to privilege resource extraction over recreation, wildlife protection, and climate-change mitigation. Richard Nixon, who in 1970 signed NEPA into law, would have been stunned by this effort to strip his landmark legislation's environmental and democratic protections.

A lawyer, Nixon might have also asked whether there is any evidence that NEPA lawsuits have halted fire-reduction harvests. In 2010, the GAO asked exactly that question, and its report revealed that only two percent of US Forest Service fire-reduction plans were litigated, with the agency winning most of them. Tossing such inconvenient truths aside, Zinke, Perdue, and Pruitt and their congressional supporters instead ratcheted up the politicized critique of NEPA. As Senator Steve Daines (R-MT) declared: "If we don't start managing our forests, the forests are going to start managing us."

The Forest Service made a similar, and costly, claim in the charred aftermath of the Big Blowup of 1910, when hurricane-force winds drove the inferno across Washington, Idaho and Montana, killing eighty-five people and charring three million acres in three days. Rather than acknowledging that weather conditions were the source of that fire's immense damage, and in knee-jerk reaction to politicians' and lumber industry's criticism that it let millions of board feet go up in smoke, the Forest Service promised to deploy all available human, fiscal, and technological resources to extinguish future outbreaks. In the 1930s, the can-do agency upped the ante, pledging to suppress all fires by ten a.m. the day after they had been reported. It deliberately ignored its own ecologists, who had concluded a decade earlier that fires were often essential to regenerating forest health. Instead, politics determined policy.

That has changed to a degree. Since the 1980s, the Forest Service has followed the lead of the National Park Service by infusing wildfire science into its firefighting strategies. As an example, look no farther than Montana's Lolo Peak fire that Zinke, *et al.* decried. Firefighters carefully managed the flames as it burned through sections of lodgepole pine, knowing that this species requires intense heat to split open its cones and release their tightly packed and resin-bound seeds, a concept called *serotiny*. So, although Zinke and crew denounced the Lolo Peak blaze as a symbol of all that is wrong with contemporary forest management, that fire actually signaled how a well-managed fire can create more resilient forests in our climate-charged era.

This is the conversation in which the Trump administration and the Republican-controlled Congress should have engaged. Giving them an unparalleled opening to do just that was the 2017 Climate Science Special Report. Its data confirmed that the earth is warmer now than it has been in 1,700 years, and that our warmer temperatures have triggered a series of extreme weather events and fueling intense wildland conflagrations. No amount of logging, scapegoating, or dismantling NEPA protections will alter the pressing, existential challenges that climate change poses.

LA is Burning!

La Tuna Canyon. Anaheim Hills. Thomas. Creek. Rye. Skirball. Each of these evocatively named fires ripped across portions Southern California during the summer and fall of 2017. Together, they consumed tens of thousands of acres and forced the evacuations of hundreds of thousands of residents. This crazed choreography of flame and people is repeated as each of these conflagrations — like countless others before them — scream over ridgelines or roar up canyons, and panicking homeowners bolt. Flames get us moving.

It's also true, however, that people have made these fires in the most fundamental sense: we bear torches. The most obvious of these torchbearers are the arsonists who take advantage of the region's desiccated and fire-prone landscapes and the intense Santa Ana winds (an example is the 2009 Station Fire, which burned 160,000 acres in the Angeles National Forest). Another and increasingly more consequential ignition source are the electrical utilities without which modern life would be less illuminated. Southern California Edison — like its southern counterpart, San Diego PG&E, and its northern, PG&E — owns substations and high-voltage transmission lines that are a towering feature of the urban landscape, and which have been implicated in nearly every major fire since 2003. Their transformers blow up, lines spark in high winds, power poles fall.

Once lit, whether by means intentional or accidental, fires gain their people-scattering force as a direct consequence of human geography, of how and where we live especially in Southern California. For more than a century, Los Angeles has pressed out from its central core. Late nineteenth-century streetcars and then automobiles facilitated this flight, a dispersal that accelerated after the 1920s, and then took off in the postwar era. Sprawl and the City of Angels became synonymous.

Between the 1950s and 1970s, new wealthy subdivisions in the Hollywood Hills, Beverly Hills, and Bel Air experienced devastating fires. Subsequent waves of exurban migration into such valleys as the San Fernando, Simi, San Gabriel, and Pomona, which flowed along the ever-expanding grid of freeways and their interlocking subdivisions (with the requisite billboard exhortation at each exit: "If You Lived Here, You'd Be Home By Now!"), produced the same smoke-filled results.

The pattern has continued apace, and Los Angeles is now the second most dense large city in the United States. This density has led those seeking more affordable housing into an ever-expanding periphery, including portions of the Mojave Desert and the northern slope of the San Gabriel Mountains. Some of these peripheral locations were among those recently engulfed in flames.

An example is the Blue Cut Fire in August 2016. Relatively small, it burned about 37,000 acres in the Cajon Pass through which Interstate 15 carries heavy commuter traffic between the inland valleys and the eastern desert. What was most striking about this particular fire was not that firefighters had to battle it amid pinball-like, powerful winds, and daytime temperatures that soared above one hundred degrees, but that it flushed more than eighty thousand people from this relatively remote and rural terrain. The periphery is getting crowded.

The next September brought more of the same. The La Tuna Canyon fire, which burned an estimated seven thousand acres in the Verdugo Mountains in northeastern Los Angeles, jumped the 210 freeway and burned the edges of numerous cul-de-sac neighborhoods. A month later, the Anaheim Hills blaze scorched eight thousand acres in Orange County, including dozens of homes crowded up this high ground. In early December, four fires erupted under extreme Santa Ana conditions. The Thomas (282,000 acres); Creek (15,000); Rye (7,000); and the tiny Skirball (475 acres) may have varied wildly in size, but like the Blue Cut they propelled massive evacuations, burned countless homes and other structures, and their toxic fumes smeared the sky.

Their physical locations are as revelatory. Each burned in and around vital highways, disrupting daily life. The Skirball hugged the 405, arguably the nation's busiest freeway. The Creek was framed to its south by the 210, hopping over it at one point). The Rye flowed along Interstate 5 and Highway 126 corridors, and the largest fire, the Thomas, not only swerved close to the 126, it burned both sides of the 33 and the 101.

The fire season used to be concentrated in the late summer and fall. Now fires flare up in any month, thanks to another anthropogenic driver: climate change. It's responsible in good measure for the bone-dry conditions accompanying the region's extended years of drought, a process that has fueled fires in Southern California and now in other areas of the West from January to December. This twelve-month cycle will hold true across the rest of the twenty-first century, too, with temperatures rising and precipitation decreasing. When these climatic conditions continue to collide with the built landscape, as they have since the beginning of the current century, the consequences will be every bit as unsettling and disastrous.

Put in context, every stretch of highway we grade, yard of concrete we pour, house we build, transmission line we hang, and mile we drive helps set the stage for these fiery dramas.

Enough is Enough

The Saddleridge Fire in Sylmar at the northern edge of Los Angeles burned for three weeks in October 2019. The latest in a long line of infernos that have chased tens of thousands of Angelenos from their homes, it disrupted the region's massive transportation grid and turned the air toxic. The Saddleridge Fire serves as a microcosm of the larger issues at stake. Keep in mind that it was the *fourth* such major conflagration to erupt in the Sylmar area in the preceding eleven years.

In November 2008, driven by eighty-mile-an-hour Santa Ana winds, the Sayre/Sylmar Fire raced through more than eleven thousand acres, roughly seventeen square miles, and shut down the five major freeways that crisscross the area—the 5, 210, 14, 405, and the 118. As astonishing as the fire's geographical reach, its flames reached fifty feet, the height of a five-story building. The Sayre/Sylmar Fire burned so hot that firefighters' hoses, laid out on concrete, melted.

Few dwellings could withstand its acetylene-torch intensity. More than six hundred homes and other structures went up in smoke, many of which were manufactured housing. The Oakridge Mobile Home Park was the site of the greatest loss, not least, as one of its residents put it, because its name was a misnomer: home to golf putting greens, an Olympic-sized swimming pool, and tennis courts, it was "the Beverly Hills of mobile homes." The fire was no respecter of the community's perceived status. The site's skeletal remains — twisted metal, piles of rubble, incinerated plants, trees, and bushes — remained visible from the 210 Freeway years later, a ghastly, ghostly reminder of this particular fire's incendiary rush that also forced more than one hundred thousand people to evacuate.

Nearly the same tragic story had played out December 2017 when the wind-whipped fifteen thousand-acre Creek Fire exploded a few miles away from where the Sylmar Fire had started. During its month-long run, the Creek Fire leaped across the same set of freeways as its embers rode the swift Santa Ana winds and set spot fires far in advance of the main blaze. Although the number of structures it consumed was far fewer than the 2008 fire — "only" 128 houses were lost — it, too, led to a massive evacuation, as more than 115,000 sought shelter from the furious firestorm.

Their flight was further complicated by the fact that the Creek Fire was just one of a devastating complex of fires that December, including the monster Thomas Fire which burned a record at the time of nearly three hundred thousand acres and killed two people. These fires, which came paired with the smaller Rye and Skirball fires, demonstrated once again the tight links between housing developments hammered into the fire zones, and the highways that enable people to commute to and from these peripheral communities. Every time a fast-moving fire roars down a canyon, flashes across a highway, or takes out the house next door, these roads become lifelines.

Understanding the context of the Saddleridge Fire is important. What would happen once the Santa Ana winds died down and firefighters had a chance to get it under control? Once extinguished, would the Saddleridge Fire lead to soul-searching in local and county governments about how their default commitment to okaying subdivisions in California's fire zones simply, clearly added fuel to an already flammable landscape? Would these public servants finally reckon with the reality that what we have been describing as wildfires are really structural fires? Or would they continue to pursue business as normal, use the state's housing crisis to sanction the construction of vast subdivisions, and hope for the best? The questions are leading, maybe even rhetorical. But then as anyone residing in Sylmar can attest, now for the fourth time, hope is not a fireproof strategy.

Hot and Fast

The Mountain View Fire, which erupted in mid-September 2020, burned an estimated 29,000 acres — twice the area of Manhattan Island — in the remote and ruggedly beautiful Eastern Sierra region along the California and Nevada border. The largest fire there in recent memory, in any other year its size and intensity would have challenged the long-held belief that the Eastern Sierra was almost fireproof. One historian dubbed the region the "asbestos" flank of the Sierra Nevada.

But this was not just any year. The Mountain View Fire, even if combined with the earlier 2020 Slink Fire, which consumed 25,000 acres, pales in comparison to the inferno-like siege that gripped California that August and September, when five of the state's six largest fires in modern history were burning simultaneously though a combined 2.4 million acres. Nearly half that figure was the result of a single fire, the August Complex. Another of these major conflagrations, the 380,000-acre Creek Fire, spewed so much toxic smoke over the Central Sierra that for a time Bishop, Mammoth Lakes, and other small Eastern Sierra communities registered some of the highest levels of air pollution in the world.

By contrast, the Mountain View Fire appeared microscopic, yet it packed a punch for the residents of the tiny towns of Walker, Topaz, and Coleville whose residents were forced to evacuate in advance of the fast-moving blaze. Many of them returned to the charred remains of their homes and other structures. And there can be no meaningful compensation for the family of the fire's one known fatality.

Even as these communities mourned their losses—human and material—this particular fire required another reckoning. Start with its location. Although the region's foothills and mountains are home to sage and pine, this beautiful land of little rain can burn every bit as hot as the dense forests on the Sierra's western slope.

The fire's timing was just as noteworthy. The Mountain View Fire blew up during the third week in November. Yes, November, weeks after the first snowfall in the area. The heat had roared back, and wind gusts hit eighty miles per hour. Although the wind speed was unusual, the eastern slope of the Sierra often experiences foehn winds. Warm, dry, and strong, they push downslope and race across the valleys below. This potent combination swiftly drove the sky-high flames through still-dry brush and forest "like a freight train," as the National Weather Service put it. The fire's crackling energy and furious run testify to the lengthening and intensifying of the fire season across the US West.

That only a day after the Mountain View Fire ignited, snow and rain began to fall within the fire's upper-elevation perimeter is consistent with a new and disturbing reality. "Whiplash weather" is the term meteorologists use to describe these rapid swings in weather patterns, from dry to wet and back again, from drought to flood. These quick oscillations driven by climate crisis complicate firefighters' strenuous efforts to control mega- and micro-fires.

Firefighting operations will become even more complex throughout the rest of the twenty-first century. Researchers predict the Sierra region, among others, will become warmer, possibly increasing by ten degrees F by 2100. If so, UCLA scientists note, a hyper-heated Sierra will bring an interlocking set of cascading effects. The snowpack will decrease markedly, the soil will be warmer, and the vegetation regardless of elevation — tree, grass, or brush — will be drier for longer periods of time. Less precipitation, hotter days and nights, and a more desiccated landscape isn't good news for firefighters or for the thousands who live in the fire zones.

The Mountain View Fire offers a chilling view of this more perilous future. It was not an aberration, the exception that proves the rule of an asbestos-sided Eastern Sierra. It was a harbinger. We had best heed the warning.

Architects of Smoke

In the summer of 2020, toxic smoke plumes darkened the skies of small Oregon communities like Bend and Sisters and those in the Eastern Sierra of California, where air quality was so bad it was reported as "beyond index." The metropolitan areas of Seattle, Portland, the San Francisco Bay Area, and Los Angeles were also blanketed in smoke. Indeed, during mid-September 2020, Portland attained the dubious honor of having the worst air pollution in the world. Seattle and the Bay Area came in second and third, and Los Angeles, while recording its worst air pollution in nearly thirty years, was a distant eighth.

We should not be surprised that the West erupted in fire. Nor that more than four million acres burned in California, another million in Oregon and in Washington State, forcing tens of thousands of people to evacuate. The downwind consequences were not a shock either.

In the end, the least remarkable thing about that summer's fierce conflagrations is that they are merely another in a string of really bad fire seasons. Sixteen of California's twenty worst fires have occurred since 2003. Worse yet: five of the largest six erupted in August and September 2020. We have done this to ourselves. We are the architects of a world of smoke.

Vividly showing this is a particularly gripping photograph from the *Los Angeles Times* that was snapped in the devastated aftermath of the 2020 Bear Fire. Subsequently subsumed into the North Complex Fire, it burned more than 250,000 acres in the Plumas National Forest. But this photograph could have been taken at any of the infernos of the summer of 2020 — or any fires before then or since. It probably has, too, because its symbolism is striking: a car resting on its buckled roof with its tires and hubcaps incinerated, body paint stripped, windows shattered, and wheels weirdly melted. In the middle ground another car, right side up but equally gutted, looks as if it has been chopshopped. Framing the backdrop is the charred, ash-white remains of a once-green Sierran forest.

Even as we fear for these abandoned automobiles' drivers and are astounded at the intensity of heat that could turn tempered steel molten, we cannot deny that burned-out cars are apt symbols for explaining the circumstances of these fires.

As soon as this four-wheeled, fossil-fueled, late-nineteenth-century technology was invented it became iconic of the Industrial Revolution, a sign of economic prosperity and accelerated mobility. But the automobile's carbon-based emissions, when combined with the release of other greenhouse gases, has raised the Earth's temperature, a planetary warming which has profoundly changed the climate.

As a result, large swaths of the West have been drying out. Since the 1980s, Colorado, New Mexico, Arizona, Utah, Nevada and California have borne the brunt of this process. According to the Palmer Drought Severity Index, the pace has quickened over the past two decades. Other Environmental Protection Agency data indicates that warmer and drier conditions will persist in the West for the rest of the twenty-first century, altering vegetation cover, endangering wildlife, and sparking a significant increase in intense fire activity. The apocalypse is anthropogenic.

That this drying out is a human construction is also hammered into every subdivision that since the 1950s has sprawled across Phoenix's Valley of the Sun and the flatlands and rumpled hills of the Bay Area, Portland, and Seattle-Tacoma. The explosive growth of these urban centers and their high-tech economies continues to energize their outward thrust, an expanding periphery that has bulldozed into canyonlands, up and over foothills, and flattened ridgelines.

Less well understood is that this rapidly evolving human geography has forged a close link between sprawl and wildland fire. Since the 1990s, for example, more than thirty-four million new households were built in western fire zones, with disastrous results. Forest Service researchers confirm this rapid infill of the wildland-urban interface—where subdivisions meet or intermix with natural areas, landscapes that more accurately should be designated "fire zones"—has been experiencing the greatest loss of life and property. More than eighty percent of all structures that burned had been constructed in areas known to burn. But what surprised these analysts was that half of the buildings that burned were located on land with the *least* natural vegetation. Forests did not surround the structures that burned. What these researchers found is that it was not simply that people were building in the fire zones, but that piles of wood stored close to homes, propane tanks fueling heating and stoves, and gas-tank vehicles were critical ignition points. Put another way, wildfires have become structural fires.

Consider Los Angeles a stand-in for the larger and unsettling western pattern. Between the 1950s and 1970s, its elite began to build mansions in Hollywood and Beverly Hills. No sooner had moguls, movie stars, and other celebrities set up house than devastating fires ripped through the new neighborhoods. One of these new residents, a tie-wearing Richard Nixon, was photographed atop his Bel Air home in 1961, hose in hand, wetting down its shake-shingled roof.

Since then, waves of ex-urban migration have flowed out along the region's expansive freeway network, whose every exit contains an interlocking set of subdivisions, gas stations, restaurants, hotels, and big-box centers. Predictably, these insta-towns have generated the same smoke-filled results. Sylmar, located in northeastern Los Angeles County, has burned repeatedly since 2008.

This pattern of build-and-burn will continue in Southern California as well as in rural areas throughout the west. City representatives and county commissioners, some cozy with the developers who underwrite their political campaigns, are quick to greenlight housing projects, even in designated fire zones. There seems to be very little political will — despite the recent fires and the charred remains of subdivisions that have fueled their energy — to halt the spread of sprawled housing slotted to be built in fire zones.

Consider the twelve-hundred-home, upscale Otay Ranch in eastern San Diego County. The county commissioners approved this development in August 2020 despite the fact that the Otay Ranch project will be constructed within an area that has burned every eighteen months for the past hundred years. Even more baffling is the gargantuan 12,000-acre planned community called Centennial that is being built in the flammable foothills of the Sierra Pelona and Tehachapi mountains in northern Los Angeles County. When completed, it will be home to sixty thousand people, many of whom will commute into Los Angeles for work along the already bumper-to-bumper Interstate 5.

What could halt this suburbanizing march into the woods throughout the West? Stronger local control over new development would be a good start, but too few communities and counties have adopted such slow-growth measures. In response to the disturbing 2020 fire season and lack of action, California's Attorney General Xavier Bacerra filed a motion in February 2021 to support a lawsuit brought by the California Native Plant Society and Center for Biological Diversity that challenged Lake County's certification of the 16,000-acre Guenoc Valley Mixed Use Planned Development. Like Otay Ranch and Centennial, the Guenoc project sits within a fire zone, which, as Bacerra pointed out, has burned eleven times since 1952, four of these blazes since 2014. "Lake County residents have borne the brunt of many of the recent wildfires that have ravaged our state," Bacerra declared. "They deserve to know that the increased wildfire risks resulting from any new development in their area have been properly considered—and mitigated." His unprecedented action may finally shock county and city governments to think twice before rubber-stamping development that endangers public health and safety and violates state environmental regulations.

In the long term, we must also reintroduce fire back to the land. Across California, for example, Indigenous Nations, often in partnership with local, state, and federal land-management agencies, have been burning to restore cultural resources. In San Diego County, the Kumeyaah have been experimenting with fire to restore watershed health and riparian habitats. For similar reasons, but on a larger scale, the Yoruk, Hupa, and Karuk are among the communities living in northern California that use controlled or prescribed fires to regain cultural and ritual resources, as well as salmon, elk, and forage plants. In the Sierras, the North Fork Mono Nation have been especially active in returning what Ron Goode, their chairman, describes as "good fire" to the foothills. "This is old land," Goode notes. "It's been in use for thousands and thousands of years. And so what we're doing out here is restoring life."

Absent this and other proactive interventions — protective and restorative — we will continue to witness summer after summer of large infernos chasing thousands of people from their homes and communities.

That is neither good public policy, nor is it smart, sustainable, or safe. Unchanged, it leaves only one option for those living in the towns and developments that encroach deep into western fire zones. To keep their vehicles gassed up and pointed downhill, with their prized possessions and go-bags handy.

UNEARTHED

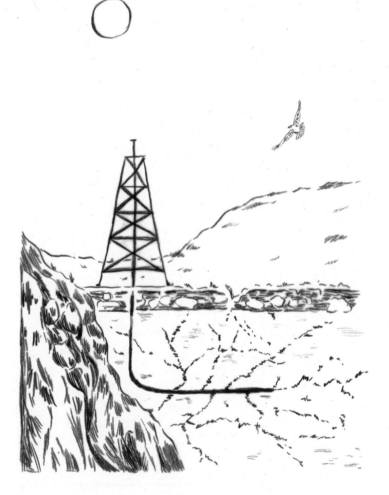

America Fracked

Three men, dressed in rumpled jeans, wrinkled T-shirts, and mud-stained boots, worked their phones in a hotel lobby in rural northeastern Pennsylvania. They were coordinating workers and material across several job sites, and during a pause in their rapid-fire conversations they started talking about the pristine quality of the local gurgling brooks and gushing streams that pour into the Delaware River on its long run to the Atlantic. It was so unlike the quality of their native Louisiana bayous and creeks, now ruined by the toxic effluent from oil rigs, gas wells, and flaring refineries. "I get why folks are fighting up here," one said. "You can see clear to the bottom."

I'd flown in from California the night before and was eating a bowl of oatmeal the next morning when this conversation unfolded in a hotel in Milford, Pennsylvania. The picturesque town is home to Grey Towers National Historic Site, the family mansion of conservationist Gifford Pinchot. I was about to head there to lead a series of workshops on the history of the Forest Service, Pinchot's efforts as its first chief, and the controversies that enveloped the agency and its inaugural leader. I immediately changed my initial talking points and used the Louisiana workers' discussion to frame the continued relevance of early twentieth-century conservation initiatives, one of which was the paired protection of watersheds and public health.

That reciprocal relationship remains central to the intense political struggle, which in 2011 dominated civic life along the Marcellus Formation, an extensive shale structure that runs underneath the Allegheny Plateau, from the Finger Lakes region in New York State south through Pennsylvania and into West Virginia. I knew enough to know that while this region is twenty-five hundred miles from home, there are similar shale formations in the Golden State containing major reserves of oil and natural gas. What was happening in the mid-Atlantic region would not, did not, stay there.

Estimated to containing between 250–500 trillion cubic feet of natural gas, "Marcellus Shale represents a ... supply that could meet America's energy needs for the next fifty to eighty years or more." That's what John W. Ubinger of the Pennsylvania Environmental Council told the US Senate Committee on the Environment and Public Works in mid-April 2011. This astronomical underground resource was what had brought the three men to that hotel lobby in Milford and why they formed part of a larger army of those seeking to tap these deep, fluid riches.

Not everyone was convinced this prospect was an unalloyed good. A determined group of older and young activists, parents and politicians were organizing to protect their rivers and aquifers from the noxious by-products such as benzene from the relatively new technique for gas extraction being used in the Marcellus called hydraulic fracturing—fracking for short.

To crack open the shale and release the natural gas trapped within, companies such as Oklahoma-based Devon Energy and Chesapeake Energy ("America's Champion of Natural Gas") drill deep into the rocky formations, inject a sand-water-and-chemical-laced fluid at high pressure to fracture the rock, allowing gas molecules to flow to the wellhead. These gas goliaths tout this fossil fuel as "clean energy," and wrap their actions in the flag (fracking = energy independence = patriotism). However, fracking could not be a dirtier source of energy.

Fracking's environmental ramifications are the shocking subject of 2010's Emmy-winning and Oscar-nominated documentary "Gasland," which exposes fracking's impact on communities across the United States. A key scene from the film shows a resident of a fracking area turn on the kitchen tap, flick a lighter, and then watch as the flowing water explode into flame from stray gas released by fracking. No amount of corporate greenwashing could scrub away that unsettling, alchemic image from the public's eye.

The *New York Times* followed up on the film's success with an in-depth exposé of the situation confronting Pennsylvania, which it dubbed "Ground Zero." Outspent and outmaneuvered, the state's regulators failed to rein in the rapid extraction process. "We simply cannot keep up," one official confessed. "There's just too much of the waste." The *Times'* exposé detailed Congress's embarrassing failure to act on the reams of evidence implicating fracking in tainting groundwater supplies in Texas, Wyoming, Colorado, California and many other states.

The *Times'* investigative report also pointed out that the nation's premiere legislation on water quality, the Safe Drinking Water Act of 1974, exempts many of the toxic materials and chemicals used in fracking from federal oversight. The exemption was a result of energy-state representatives ramming through a 2005 amendment to the Act [section 142(d)] that explicitly provided such protective cover. No wonder the US Environmental Protection Agency was unable to crack down on this dangerous technology.

In the resulting political vacuum, informal groups formed up and down the Allegheny Plateau, across the Plains states, the Intermountain West, and the West Coast, to force the issue on their state legislatures. They have made no headway in West Virginia, and the outcome was little better in Pennsylvania, where more than fourteen hundred wells already had been drilled when "Gasland" first aired. Discouragingly, the next year the Keystone State issued more than thirty-three hundred additional permits.

The one political success occurred in New York, where state legislators banned fracking. As important as that legislation was, subsequent events have demonstrated a state-by-state strategy can't win the day. As with other reform movements in US history — antislavery, women's suffrage, and civil rights — such local agitation must be accompanied with state *and* national legislative action. Bottom-up pressure must fuse with top-down force.

Enter California's senators, Barbara Boxer and Dianne Feinstein. Starting in 2010, they repeatedly co-sponsored various iterations of the Fracturing Responsibility and Awareness of Chemicals (FRAC) Act. As Boxer pointed out in a letter to her constituents that year, this legislation if passed, "would have amended the Safe Drinking Water Act to repeal such exemptions for fracking. The FRAC Act would have required oil and gas companies to disclose the chemicals they use in the process."

This latter requirement is crucial. Without complete disclosure from this unusually secretive industry, neither the EPA nor the public can accurately determine fracking's carcinogenic potential, nor how much it has already polluted America's groundwater and surface water. We don't know how much this pollution has compromised public health, safety, and welfare.

The California senators' support is not simply a sympathetic gesture for those elsewhere who are currently wrestling with the consequences of fracking. Feinstein and Boxer recognized that their state was already a battleground.

In 2010, for example, the Monterey County zoning administrator signed off on a permit for Venoco, a Colorado outfit, to employ fracking techniques to drill nine exploratory oil wells in Hames Valley in the county's southern reach, roughly halfway between San Francisco and Santa Barbara. Immediately appealing the decision was the Ventana Conservation and Land Trust. At the same time, the US Bureau of Land Management, which manages all subsurface mineral rights on federal property, admitted that an oil company, which it refused to identify, expressed interest in leasing more than two thousand acres of federal land over the same shale formation.

Then came news that Venoco had been fracking in two wells located on private land in northern Santa Barbara County. When county supervisors, like their colleagues in Monterey, tried to secure information from the company about its actions locally, Venoco stonewalled. "This has been in the news a lot lately," noted supervisor Doreen Farr, "and I think a simple information presentation would be beneficial to both the board and the public."

Ever since, there have been additional dismissals of the public's right to know, as other oil-and-gas conglomerates continue fracking in a mad-dash effort to flush fossil fuels out of deep shale deposits in California. Every denial has added fuel to the opposition, which includes an intersecting set of environmental-justice advocates concerned with the disproportionate burden that less-wealthy, mostly nonwhite communities bear as a result of fracking in the extensive oil-and-gas fields in Kern, Santa Barbara, and Los Angeles counties. They have been joined by other environmental organizations and several stalwart legislators in Sacramento, all propelled by the worry that if they cannot rein in fracked production then the California's unspoiled waterways and clean aquifers will become as compromised as those in Louisiana and Pennsylvania.

At Fault

There is nothing mysterious about the appeal of hydraulic fracturing, the earth-shaking technique that cracks open deep, tight shale formations to release trapped oil and gas. It makes a lot of money—for companies involved in the production processes, for state treasurers collecting taxes, for those lucky enough to own the mineral rights beneath their property. Anecdotes abound of immense energy business profits wrung from fracking, and of instant multi-millionaires in formerly cash-strapped parts of south Texas, central Pennsylvania, and North Dakota.

These narratives of Capitalism Triumphant make for good copy. No less compelling is the inverse: this boom will crash. When the bust comes, and it's already started in some places because of low oil prices, the very communities benefiting the most from fracking fields like the Eagle Ford Play in the Lone Star State, the Keystone State's Marcellus Formation, or the Baaken Formation in the Peace Garden State will be in serious trouble. This narration comes with an accompanying I-told-you-so proverb, especially relevant to those living in these once-hardscrabble agricultural regions: you reap what you sow.

California Assemblyman Richard Bloom was among those hoping to fend off such a harrowing harvest. He represents a pretty tony legislative district, the 50th, stretching from Malibu to Hollywood and encompassing the gilded communities of Brentwood, Bel Air, and Beverly Hills, and a constituency that is nicely insulated from the state's oil-and-gas patch. But in February 2013, he submitted legislation to prohibit fracking operations. Until, that is, "the Legislature enacts subsequent legislation that determines whether and under what conditions hydraulic fracturing may be conducted." His bill, AB 1301, cleared the Assembly's Natural Resources Committee but ultimately stalled.

The central thrust of his legislative initiative was to "protect the public health and safety and the natural resources of the state." It would also stay in effect until the Natural Resources Agency and the Department of Conservation's Division of Oil, Gas, and Geothermal Resources (DOGGR), which is responsible for providing oil and gas well permits, develops the necessary regulatory framework to assess, monitor, and control fracking in California.

What was of considerable concern to Bloom and his colleagues Holly Mitchell (D-Culver City), Adrin Nazarian (D-East Fernando Valley), and Senator Fran Pavley (D-Agoura Hills), was that no one knows the extent to which this technology is being employed in California. "State regulators have little knowledge of what chemicals have been used," Bloom observed at the time. "They cannot notify people if fracking is occurring in their communities and are unable to determine if fracking is polluting groundwater or impacting air quality."

This ignorance is disconcerting because of fracking's deleterious impact on air and water quality in other states. The latter is especially concerning in the oft-arid west. In Webb County, Texas, for instance, researchers estimate the amount of water used for fracking represents as much as one-third of the area's annual groundwater recharge, the amount of surface water that percolates back to the underground aquifer supplying the region.

Add to those hidden costs the unmistakably potholed road systems that come with fracking. Dangerous, high-speed trucks pound back roads and farm-to-market arterials. This transportation system is ill-equipped to handle the damaging weight and volume of traffic, and the corresponding high level of collisions and overturns.

Fracking's association with earthquakes is also driving the need for effective legislation, a reasonable response in a landscape with as much seismic activity as California. The fracking industry routinely dismisses claims that its operations trigger active faults or reactivate dormant ones, and brushes aside research indicating that its waste-water injection wells contribute to increased seismic activity. However, its casual disregard for a growing scientific literature was much harder to maintain in the face of peer-reviewed reports from USGS researchers. Their baseline research in the Raton Basin in New Mexico, which established a clear link between the use of waste-water injection wells and the rapid rise in temblors in northeastern New Mexico and southern Colorado. Noting there have been twenty times the number of magnitude-3 or larger quakes between 2001 and 2011 than in the preceding three decades, the largest of which was a 5.3 temblor in 2011,

Jason Rubenstein, a USGS geophysicist, asked: "Can this rate of change be natural? I certainly don't think so."

Accelerating anxiety in California are reports that prospecting firms are scrutinizing the Monterey Shale deposit, a geological formation that extends from northern California to the Southland, which the industry claims to contain two-thirds of all the known recoverable oil in the continental United States. Fracking is already being conducted within this play, the *New York Times* reported in February 2013, and there was a spike in the number of bidders for leases on federal land and the prices they were willing to pay. "Some of that has to do with speculation on new technologies," a Bureau of Land Management agent said, "and some of that has to do with the high price of oil."

This evidence increased local and regional demand for state oversight. Governor at the time, Jerry Brown, was unwilling to press this case, and the regulatory agencies hadn't announced a clear-cut set of rules to control the impact of hydraulic fracturing on public health and the environment. That's what led a bevy of legislators to produce a series of bills, although Senator Pavley's bill, SB 4, was the only one to make it to the governor's desk. He signed off, even as Pavley called SB 4 a "compromise" bill. It didn't shut down fracking operations but required the state's Natural Resources Agency to complete a scientific study of the technology's ramifications by 2015 and compelled the industry to notify state agencies of the precise formulas of their injection fluids.

This half-a-loaf strategy didn't appease Assemblyman Bloom, whose bill requiring an immediate moratorium failed to advance in the legislature. "We need a reality check," the Santa Monica legislator asserted. "There is no requirement for the regulatory process to be completed by next spring and given the snail's pace to date ... I have little confidence in the State's ability to stick to its timeline." Only the passage of a tough-love prohibition embedded in his legislation, AB 1301, "will incentivize all stakeholders to address the public health, safety, and environmental hazards that fracking poses to California."

A California Nightmare

Benzene is back was the grim news in February 2015. Drawing on analyses that the Center for Biological Diversity had conducted, Julie Cart, an investigative journalist for the *Los Angeles Times*, reported that "significant concentrations" of benzene, a cancer-causing petroleum derivative, had been found in fracking waste liquid in California.

How significant? Cart noted that "benzene levels thousands of times greater than state and federal agencies consider safe" have been identified, a chilling identification because since the late nineteenth century benzene has been directly linked to aplastic anemia and leukemia. Benzene is a killer.

But it's not the only toxin injected into the state's fracking waste-disposal wells. Disturbingly high levels of chromium 6 were detected, upwards of 2,700 times the recommended level established by the state's Office of Environmental Health Hazard Assessment. The chemical may cause an increase in cancers and harm the reproductive system. Toluene, which is known to compromise the central nervous system and harm developing fetuses, also registered at abnormally high levels.

These findings only came to light because of the 2013 passage of SB4, which requires energy companies to test and report the chemical composition of the fluids injected into waste wells. The data led the Environmental Protection Administration as well as state agencies to argue that toxic fluid disposal constitutes a serious violation of clean water regulations and poses a distinct threat to public health.

They are right to be worried. With upwards of 700,000 waste injection wells nationwide, and multiplying as fracking accelerated across the country, questions mounted about the accuracy of the science that supported this form of waste removal. ProPublica, the investigative journalism organization, probed this issue in 2012 and reported the following:

The boom in oil and natural gas drilling is deepening the uncertainties, geologists acknowledge. Drilling produces copious amounts of waste, burdening regulators and demanding hundreds of additional disposal wells. Those wells — more holes punched in the ground — are changing the earth's geology, adding man-made fractures that allow water and waste to flow more freely.

Hydrogeologist Stefan Finsterle of the Lawrence Berkeley National Laboratory put it bluntly: "There is no certainty at all in any of this, and whoever tells you the opposite is not telling you the truth. You have changed the system with pressure and temperature and fracturing, so you don't know how it will behave."

None of this shocked long-time anti-fracking activists. They had pushed hard for legislation to stop hydraulic fracturing in the Golden State because they were deeply concerned about its impact on groundwater supplies, including essential aquifers. Arguing that the data reveals a statewide "disaster," what really concerned Hollin Kretzmann, an attorney for the Center for Biological Diversity, was the incompleteness of the SB4 data.

"They are trying to piece it all together—in some cases decades after these injections started." The "they" is the Division of Oil, Gas and Geothermal Resources (DOGGR), the state agency charged with overseeing energy production.

The agency's oversight had been slipshod. According to the Center and the *Los Angeles Times* DOGGR failed to post on its website required test results from at least a hundred wells, among other lapses. "Central Valley water officials also recently revealed that at least 383 oil industry wastewater pits are operating without permits or oversight," the Center for Biological Diversity confirmed. "Most wastewater pits are unlined and don't have covers"—all violations of state law. So egregious were DOGGR's failures that even the EPA, not known for its willingness to rein in Big Oil & Gas, chastised its lax approach to regulation.

That a regulatory agency could be so negligent ought to be unimaginable. But it's not. There's a long history of federal and state agencies being captured by the very industries that they are supposed to regulate. Historian Gabriel Kolko exposed this process in his 1963 book, *The Triumph of Conservatism*, which details a corporatist nation-state in which big business and big government formed a powerful, mutually self-interested coalition. During the Progressive Era, Kolko asserted, efforts to control the meatpacking, steel, and copper industries came not from grassroots activists but from major corporations who wrote the relevant statutes so that they could control legal oversight and crush their competition.

The enduring power of Kolko's insights into how political capitalism operates is reflected in subsequent analyses of the old Atomic Energy Commission (now the Nuclear Regulatory Commission) and state public utility commissions, many of whose personnel also come from the industries that they are charged with overseeing. Californians know all about the impact that such revolving doors can have. Michael Peevey, the former president of Southern California Edison, and later the disgraced head of the state's Public Utilities Commission, was forced out of office in 2014 after evidence piled up that he was in cahoots with his former employer and Pacific Gas & Electric, including making backdoor deals and recommending PG&E employee promotions.

Although there was no indication that DOGGR failed to protect public health due to its complicit relations with energy companies, if there's any distillate that must be scrupulously—nay, zealously—managed, it's benzene. Synthesized from coal in the nineteenth century, and now a petroleum byproduct, benzene has been used extensively as an industrial solvent. No sooner was its production ramped up than its health consequences emerged. "In those countries where benzene came to be made and used on a more industrial scale," SUNY-Stony Brook historian Chris Sellers wrote in *Global Environment,* "acute poisoning began turning up, as well as a more chronic form of poisoning. Yet only after World War I would a common pattern of chronic effect earn its own name ('aplastic anemia') and the first cases of benzene-associated leukemia show up in medical journals."

Strikingly, European health officials immediately drew a direct connection between benzene and a variety of fatal or degenerative maladies. French and German authorities named a prevalent blood disease "benzene leukemia," calling it "a disease with its presumed occupational cause."

Although US researchers had access to European medical studies that demonstrated this ineluctable connection and were reproducing the same results in their stateside laboratories, it took decades before they were willing to acknowledge what their continental colleagues took as a given. Their reluctance, Sellers observes, was a result of this nation's failure systematically to collect and analyze public medical records across the wider population and American scientists' faith in "lab-inspired epidemiology." Such research often requires outside funding from corporations. This dependency "made any claims about occupational causes — and the claimants — more vulnerable to attack by industrial interests."

German chemist Wilhelm Hueper found this out the hard way. While working for the US chemical giant DuPont, he studied workers who fabricated aniline. The volatile compound, which smells like rotten fish, is used in rubber processing, herbicide production, and dye manufacture. Hueper was one of the first to identify the chemical as a toxic substance and a carcinogen. DuPont promptly fired him.

Muzzling in-house critics has been industry standard ever since. This has had a chilling effect externally, too. Even when President Richard Nixon signed 1970 legislation creating the EPA and OSHA, the Occupational Safety and Health Administration, these new agencies' watchdog status did not shelter their analysts from outside pressure. Witness the inability, perhaps even unwillingness, of the EPA to effectively challenge the fracking industry. Lacking congressional and White House support to regulate its actions, given the putative need to secure "energy independence," the EPA has stood on the sidelines.

States have also been ineffective. Pennsylvania, Texas, and North Dakota, where fracking has been a massive presence, have refused to enact controls that would protect local water supplies. Why bite the rich hand that feeds you? Even progressive California was unwilling to take an aggressive action against the energy industry. It took a furious fight to secure SB 4, which is the state's first attempt at regulating fracking. But many activists, in response to industry lobbyists' ability to water down its final draft, refused to support the legislation. The *Los Angeles Times* concurred, editorializing in September 2013: "at this point SB 4 is so flawed that it would be better to kill it and press for more serious legislation next year."

Yet it's also true that without SB 4's reporting requirements no one in the state would have known that benzene, chromium 6, and toluene have been injected into hundreds of wastewater injection wells. No one would have known the level of threat that these toxins posed to groundwater supplies. By its reporting requirements, SB 4 energized the demands of those calling on the governor and DOGGR to do their jobs.

Divest Now

Our carbon footprint is everywhere, in the food we eat, the clothes we wear, and the spaces in which we work and sleep. It fuels all forms of modern transportation—cars, trucks, trains, buses, planes, and ships—and its residue adds toxins to the air we breathe and the water we drink.

Because extraordinary profits are wrung from exploiting carbon energy resources, mega-corporations are imploding mountaintops and drilling, fracking, and blasting ever deeper into the earth to tap fossilized riches. Those who control their production, distribution, and consumption shape deliberations from town halls to the United Nations.

Extracting ourselves, our communities, and politics from this oil-and-gas juggernaut is not going to be easy. This difficulty explains why so few immediately jump at the chance to divest their investments in such corporations as Exxon or Shell, Valero, or BP. Divestment's appeal, however, is that it helps us acknowledge our collective complicity in and our shared responsibility for a warming Earth, this imperiled planet.

"The fossil fuel industry is a rogue industry," climate activist Bill McKibben argues. "We stand to emit five times as much CO_2 as even the most conservative government says is safe. The fuel will definitely be burned unless we change the story line." How do we change that narrative? We can start by altering the character and tone of public discourse about the hegemonic clout of fossil fuels.

The motive for doing so has not and will not be the miraculous result of the ongoing climate-change conferences in Copenhagen, Mexico City, or Doha, and a host of other glamorous sites. Despite their glitter, the conferences have produced little in the way of real results. Legislative action is essential, but as the battle over fracking in the United States reveals, the well-funded opposition to the imposition of tough regulations makes it a long and compromised path to reform.

Pressure from the bottom up is therefore increasingly necessary. Divestment is one of these grassroot tactics. No surprise, then, that since around 2012 it has been a rallying cry on campuses across the country with students, staff, and faculty addressing the economic, moral, and political implications of their institutions' profitable investment in fossil fuels.

With the goal of recalculating the terrifying math of the climate crisis — we must burn less carbon-based fuel to keep global temperatures from rising more than two-degrees Celsius — 350. org, the climate crisis awareness organization, has targeted the two hundred energy companies controlling the largest oil-and-gas reserves around the world, in which are buried an estimated 2,795 gigatons of carbon. A single gigaton is one billion tons, or twice the weight of all the people on earth. 350.org's strategy has been to persuade trustees and administrations at institutions of higher education to sell their shares in carbon-based energy firms.

In one sense this is a symbolic strike considering the impact that such divestment might produce. Even if every college and university dumped Exxon, for example, it would not cripple that massive corporation. Neither would it mean that these colleges and universities would achieve fossil-fuel freedom or carbon neutrality. All travel to and from these campuses, all food brought to their loading docks, all heat, light, and other resources that warm classrooms, illuminate athletic contests, and power laboratories would remain largely carbon-based.

So, what is the point of demanding full and complete divestment? On the one hand, it offers a direct, sustained, and critical challenge to our longstanding and dangerous public silence about climate change and the threat it poses to all life on this warming planet. At once symbolic and sensible, it's also rhetorical and tactical.

On the other hand, divestment also gains legitimacy because it's historically grounded. Think of the political tactics that William Lloyd Garrison adopted in 1831 to jolt awake the somnolent abolitionist movement. Well aware that King Cotton dominated global trade in the early nineteenth century, hyper-alert to the plantation south's claim that slavery was essential to the production of this white gold, and conscious of how this export crop and the brutal labor practices that generated it was responsible for the new nation's booming economy, Garrison did not hesitate to attack this status quo precisely because it was omnipotent and omnipresent.

His demand for immediate emancipation of all slaves was blunt. "I will be as harsh as truth, and as uncompromising as justice. On this subject, I do not wish to think, or speak, or write with moderation," Garrison editorialized in January 1831 in the first issue of the *Liberator*. "No! No! Tell a man whose house is on fire, to give a moderate alarm: tell him to moderately rescue his wife from the hands of the ravisher; tell the mother to gradually extricate her babe from the fire into which it has fallen; — but urge me not to use moderation in a cause like the present. I am in earnest — I will not equivocate — I will not excuse — I will not retreat a single inch — *and I will be heard.*"

Like a lightning bolt, his words cracked through the silence that enveloped slavery's presence in the American Republic. They blew apart his fellow citizens' willingness to quietly sanction the peculiar institution that besmirched the notion that all men are created equal.

Yet Garrison recognized that his booming rhetoric and the powerful movement it engendered would not reach quick resolution. "Urge immediate abolition as earnestly as we may," he wrote in the *Liberator* in August 1831, "it will alas! be gradual abolition in the end. We have never said that slavery would be overthrown by a single blow; that it ought to be we shall always contend."

Had Garrison, Frederick Douglas, the Grimke sisters, and a host of other radical abolitionists not demanded immediate liberation, had they not pushed, cajoled, demanded, and upset their contemporaries it would have been impossible for Americans to imagine a world in which slavery did not exist. Without Garrison, in short, there would be no Lincoln. Without the Liberator there would be no Emancipation Proclamation.

Absent 350.org, and similar such groups, and by extension there would be no contemporary arena in which to debate the inimical impact of fossil fuels on our daily lives and in the body politic. There would be little pressure to make the moral choices that would align the reality of this world with the idealized vision of a carbon-free society.

There also would be much less appreciation for the cross-generational responsibility we bear so that those who will inherit this Earth can live within its sustaining embrace. To understand why, note the differing reactions of Thomas Jefferson and Theodore Roosevelt to the great crises that defined their eras.

The Master of Monticello did not need William Lloyd Garrison to tell him that slavery destroyed slave and slaveholder alike. But neither did Jefferson, whose galvanizing rhetoric in the Declaration of Independence about humanity's right to "life, liberty, and the pursuit of happiness," choose to liberate those he willingly enslaved.

He would let others lift that bale. "I am sensible of the partialities with which you have looked towards me as the person who should undertake this salutary but arduous work," the former president wrote a young friend in 1814, but "this enterprise is for the young; for those who can follow it up, and bear it through to its consummation. It shall have all my prayers, & these are the only weapons of an old man." Because he disarmed himself, Jefferson must be held partly responsible for the bloody Civil War that consumed the rising generation.

Roosevelt, whose cohort confronted the pernicious impact of an industrializing economy, refused to offload his obligations on those who later would come of age. As he and his progressive peers fought against child labor, demanded better housing, battled for universal suffrage, and defended wildlands, parks, and forests, they did so because they were convinced that they must repair a broken world in their lifetimes. "Our duty to the whole, including the unborn generations," Roosevelt asserted, "bids us restrain an unprincipled present-day minority from wasting the heritage of these unborn generations."

The same principled commitment has driven divestment activists to speak out about our collective responsibilities for the fossil fuel-driven changes rapidly altering this good earth. From such provocation comes action.

Carbon Sequestered

Progress. It can have some unusual prods, a sense of urgency that might converge with other pressures that in another time and place might not have coalesced to impel action. This may explain California Governor Gavin Newsom's announcement in late April 2021 that the state would ban the issuance of new permits for hydraulic fracturing, fracking, by January 2024. Widely praised for his decisive action, Newsom's assertion of executive authority was also puzzling: six months earlier, in October 2020, he had asserted that he did not have the unilateral power to prohibit fracking in the state.

What changed? It's not incidental that the moratorium was announced amid a recall election. Few pundits believed the GOP-led effort will succeed in driving Newsom from office — the Democratic Party had an advantage at the polls, and the Republican contenders gained little traction — it made sense for the governor to try to shore up his progressive flank. After all, grassroots organizations have been hyper-active in the state's oil patch — in Kern and Monterey, as well as Los Angeles, Orange, Ventura, and Santa Barbara counties. Since at least 2012 they've been demanding a moratorium as a critical first step to defend their communities' public health and safety. Newsom's predecessor, Jerry Brown, had stiff-armed these advocates even as he signed SB 4 that placed some constraints on fracking operations and opened the door for greater transparency about their toxicity. Newsom had been happy to follow suit, which is why in October he kicked the issue over to the legislature, deferring to its bill-writing power.

The moratorium, for all its importance, is not the end game. It doesn't stop current oil-and-gas operations and so won't resolve the befouling of the air, soil, and water that the industry has generated since some of the first rudimentary wells were hand-dug in the city of Los Angeles in 1892. Neither will it fix the many abandoned wellheads and brownfields, contaminated land, that litter such urban locations such as Signal Hill in Long Beach and Baldwin Hills in Los Angeles. Some more rural areas are in even worse shape. A *Los Angeles Times* investigative report in early 2020 revealed that there are more than 35,000 idled wells in the state, which was bad news for those who resided nearby. More than 350,000 Californians live within six hundred feet of an unplugged well, the *Times* reported. One particularly vulnerable community is Arvin, in Kern County, which has the dubious distinction, according to the EPA, of suffering from the worst smog in the nation. Some of the pollution, a toxic blend of benzene, formaldehyde, and methane, is flowing out of hundreds unplugged wells. The largely Latino town has become a major sacrifice zone, a marker of the some of the cruelest forms of environmental injustice.

To clean up Arvin and too many places like it will require billions of dollars. "All they want to do is rape the land and leave," state senator Hannah-Beth Jackson, a Santa Barbara Democrat, told the *Times.* "They are taking the resources of California, monetizing them and leaving us with the mess." While the state wrangles with the fossil-fuel industry to pay for the damages it produced, an achingly slow process, on-the-ground forces push all levels of government to enact legislation to correct some of the most immediately egregious issues. To shutter operations like those savaging Arvin, and that particularly envelop low-income and communities of color, led state assembly representative Al Muratsuchi to sponsor legislation calling for 2500-foot setback between wellfields and homes, hospitals, schools, and nursing homes; "we cannot fight systemic racism without environmental justice," he argued. Although this initiative failed in the state senate, activists at the same time were negotiating with city councils and county governments to develop local setback ordinances. Here there was greater success, particularly with an innovative strategy that coupled setbacks with a just-transition approach to the closing down and rehabbing of production sites. Los Angeles County supervisors, for one, signed off on the creation of a task force focused on plugging and remediating unproductive wells in unincorporated sections of the county. Noted Monica Embrey, an associate director for the Sierra Club's Beyond Dirty Fuels Campaign, the supervisors' "historic vote advances a just transition as a critical component to addressing the intersecting issues of climate justice, economic justice, and public health." Perhaps the most compelling aspect of the initiative is the broad coalition that supported it, which included labor unions. Who is better positioned to remediate oil-and-gas operations than those who had helped build and maintain these facilities? A question that Supervisor Mark Ridley-Thomas asked when he argued that establishing the task force offered an unparalleled opportunity "to wed our environmental goals with a meaningful workforce agenda." Progress.

WATERSHEDS

Upper Reaches

Promise a bunch of environmental historians a chance to escape the Conference Indoors for the Great Outdoors, and they will pile into a bus without a moment's hesitation. The ride becomes an elixir of sorts. The decibels increase with every mile gained, and ours was an hour-long riot of sound — shades of a high school field trip. Our destination this particular year was the Arrowrock Dam, slotted at the confluence of the main stem of the Boise River and its south fork. At one time this massive concrete arch, completed in 1915, and managed by the US Bureau of Reclamation, was the highest in the world, topping out at 348 feet. We were supposed to have a full-on tour by bureau staff, but that failed to materialize for whatever reason.

No great loss. As we walked around the site, a number of our peers, water experts all, shared their insights into the dam's rapid construction and the dangers that resulted, including the deaths of twelve workers. The dam's size and award-winning design created a vast reservoir of an estimated 286,000 acre-feet. An acre-foot supplies about three families with a year's water. The Arrowrock storage volume helps irrigate nearly four hundred thousand acres in southwestern Idaho and eastern Oregon, a welcome prospect for those seeking a consistent supply in a region that annually receives a mere twelve inches of precipitation. As one historian of the federal agency observed: Arrowrock made the desert bloom.

The bus ride back to Boise was a lot quieter. I even got in a quick nap before snapping awake when I realized I hadn't asked what the relationship was between the dam and reservoir and the larger Boise National Forest that wraps around it. I asked those on the bus, but no one knew the answer. I spent that evening digging into relevant online archives and came away with a puzzle. In a table buried in the Final Report of the National Forest Reservation Commission (1976), there were two references to land acquisitions under the heading of "Arrowrock" spread across three Idaho counties and all located in the Boise-Snake watershed. One purchase unit totaled 25,148 acres at a cost of $87,787; the second totaled 36,834 acres for $131,235. The data itself wasn't puzzling; it was the funding mechanism that startled me.

The Commission, which was created under the Weeks Act (1911), was authorized to purchase land from willing sellers in watersheds in the *eastern* half of the United States, land that would be folded into the national-forest system. The Weeks Act outlays were central to the expansion of the Boise National Forest to protect tributaries whose streamflow pooled behind the Arrowrock Dam. But also in California, its funds purchased more than 100,000 acres in the Tahoe National Forest, 22,000 in the Sequoia, and 14,000 in the Northern Redwood Purchase Unit in the Trinity National Forest—and an array of smaller sites throughout the state. These purchases only underscored how little I knew about this congressional initiative or its impact on the nation writ large.

Apparently, I wasn't alone. I anxiously queried my bus mates the next day, and they too were confounded. Phew. To be fair, few

Americans have ever heard of the Weeks Act or its transformative power on the land and in our lives. As the legislation's complex history reveals, the act, along with the remarkable activism and strategic insights of its proponents, may guide our responses to the daunting challenges we must address as the planet warms and the climate shifts.

The act's most obvious influence is reflected in the purchase of millions of acres of national forests in twenty-six eastern states. Its economic impact in terms of forestry has been immeasurable, the recreational dollars it generates even more substantial. For the millions of visitors who annually hunt, fish, hike, camp, and just plain enjoy themselves on these public lands in the Great Lakes and Plains, along the Ohio River Valley, along the Appalachians and across the south, as well as those who frolic in the Sierra or in the southern California ranges, including the Santa Ana, San Bernardino and San Gabriels, this legislative initiative is of inestimable value.

The act has also been of unparalleled political significance. For the first time, the federal government gained the authority to purchase private land in the eastern United States to create new national forests, the first of which was North Carolina's Pisgah National Forest in 1916. But it could only do so within the context of cooperative relations between Washington and the various states. The bill's long title makes this clear: "AN ACT to enable any State to cooperate with any other State or States, or with the United States, for the protection of the watersheds of navigable streams, and to appoint a commission for the acquisition of lands for the purpose of conserving the navigability of navigable rivers." This insistence on collaboration — for watershed and fire protection, especially — is one of the Weeks Act's groundbreaking qualities.

Another key feature is embodied in the text's mysterious phrase that twists the tongue: "the navigability of navigable waters." In popular culture this term signified that a stream was navigable if it could float a small log, but in this specific case the concept identified which lands the federal government could purchase and for what purposes. The act targeted high-country watersheds of rivers crossing state boundaries and linked watershed protection to the "Commerce Clause" of the US Constitution, which had granted the federal government the responsibility to regulate interstate commerce. Through the act this regulatory power was extended to interstate streamflow.

Those who pushed for the act, named for its savvy congressional floor manager, John W. Weeks (R-MA), couldn't know their initiative would have such far-reaching consequences. All they wanted was federal protection of the Appalachian Mountains. Southern conservationists, for instance, were deeply worried that heavy logging was destroying the verdant beauty of the Great Smoky Mountains or ruining the soils and intensifying flood damage along the Monongahela River. New England activists shared their concerns about the impact of deforestation on rampaging floods on the Merrimack and Connecticut rivers and damaging fires in the White Mountains. Independently, these groups lobbied for congressional legislation to create national forests, such as already existed throughout the American West.

Yet because the federal government owned almost no land in the east—which was in sharp contrast to its ownership pattern in the west—the only way it could manage eastern forests was if it bought them. Whether it had the constitutional right to buy private property was hotly debated in Congress, an argument that western politicians repeatedly raised. They were used to attacking the national forests in their region, forever challenging the Forest Service's ability to regulate the public domain and saw no reason to strengthen the agency's land inventory, budgetary allocation, or legal authority. Their hostility was one reason why the act, an early version of which had been introduced in 1900, took so long to become law.

What finally broke this legal logjam was the previously mentioned idea of "the navigability of navigable waters." In granting the federal government authority over interstate waters the bill also gave it the right to buy the land necessary to protect those waters. That language apparently mollified some of the California delegation: its two senators, Frank Flint and George Perkins voted aye. However, only two of its eight House members — including its sole Los Angeles representative, James McLachlan of Pasadena — voted in support.

These high-level legislative maneuverings wouldn't have succeeded without a broad and diverse coalition of local interests demanding the act's passage. In the south, the Appalachian National Forest Association (founded in 1899) led the way. The two key northern proponents were the Appalachian Mountain Club (1876) and the Society for the Protection of New Hampshire Forests (1901). These groups gained considerable support in California, via the Sierra Club. Without their indefatigable coalition building, and persistent lobbying in public meetings, congressional hearings, and through the media, we would not have fifty-two eastern national forests. Neither could we enjoy those acres the act purchased in southwestern Idaho, Northern and Southern California, and in other western high ground.

Without these acquisitions, our watersheds would be less green, potable water less pure, scenic vistas less stunning, and economic life less vibrant.

The act has another lesson to impart. As they fought to secure its passage, a bipartisan coalition forged long-lasting public-private partnerships that depended on an energetic and engaged citizenry. These groups were able to respond creatively and successfully to what they perceived to be the environmental challenge of their lifetime. Surely that holds true today as we attempt to build a more sustainable society amid the powerful forces that climate change has unleashed.

Another point was driven home at a subsequent environmental history conference field trip. This one, which I organized in 2018 at the Claremont Colleges, was a pre-conference event that introduced my colleagues to our library's vast water archives. Local Tongva elder Julia Bogany identified the Tongva's longstanding cosmological relationship with water as a wellspring of all life, as a sacred pulse and heartbeat. With special-collection librarians as our guides, we dipped into documents, blueprints, correspondence, and other records that demonstrated how irrigation companies, investment schemes, and public agencies transformed water into a controlled and regulated commodity.

The day ended with a tour of the Chino Basin Water Conservation District. Founded by orchard and dairy owners in the mid-twentieth century worried about conserving and regenerating finite and vulnerable water resources, the district maintains its mission through a clever use of abandoned quarries to percolate water into local aquifers. Their adaptive strategy was consistent with a charge President Theodore Roosevelt laid down while stumping for the Weeks Act. At a meeting of the Southern Conservation Congress, he urged his audience "to profit from the mistakes made elsewhere ... and so handle [natural resources] that you leave your land as a heritage to your children, increased and not impaired in permanent value."

Water Beneath Our Feet

In oft-dry Southern California, it's easy to forget we live in a series of watersheds. Then come winter storms that can slam into the San Gabriel and San Bernardino Mountains. Water roars into creeks and rivers. Mudslides barrel down hillsides. The scent of yucca, sagebrush, and buckwheat fills the air.

Yet these seemingly unmistakable signs that we live within a natural system designed to capture precipitation and move it downstream until, ultimately, some of it flows into the ocean, are not as obvious to twenty-first century inhabitants of Southern California as they were to earlier residents of this landscape. They should be. For to live more sustainably in a region buffeted by deluge and drought, we must take better care of the very watersheds that for too long we have neglected.

The Indigenous People who have lived in these valleys for millennia knew why watersheds matter. Their villages were constructed close enough to rivers, creeks and streams to readily access potable water and the plants and animals that also utilized these waterways, yet set back enough to avoid floodwaters' ravaging power.

The Spanish missions partially replicated this strategy if only because they were often sited near these Indigenous settlements, a pattern largely recapitulated during Mexican rule. The third wave of settler-colonists began to alter this dynamic. In the traumatic aftermath of the Mexican American War, a large number of Americans surged into the region and were determined to put their stamp on the land and its resources, dispossessing their predecessors from their home ground.

As part of that violent estrangement, the new migrants reconstructed the ground itself. Unlike earlier generations, they had no interest in integrating themselves into local watersheds. Wanting to build everywhere, which unrestrained floods would not allow, they used dams, culverts, and channels — and astonishing amounts of concrete — to bend nature to their will.

The same engineering mindset that bottled up the Los Angeles River, preventing it from recharging its aquifers and rebuilding its beaches, drove the decision to stream vast quantities of imported water into Southern California. The Los Angeles Aqueduct (1913), Colorado Aqueduct (1941) and State Water Project (1960) capture precipitation falling on both slopes of the Sierra as well as the western slope of the Rockies, and then sluice them into the region's life and economy. The cracks in this system have become all-too obvious during intense drought years and related spikes in the cost of imported water. Our way forward begins by looking back.

Although we are too many and too sprawled to live as lightly as the Indigenous People have in what is now known as California, we can embrace their enduring insights about the vital interconnections between mountain, canyon, wash and aquifer. Indeed, a century ago, a few white settlers took their ideas to heart. In the Pomona Valley, for example, citrus growers collaborated with local governments in developing a unique system for infiltrating surface water into the aquifer below. They set aside "spreading grounds" to allow water flowing out of San Antonio Canyon — the Mount Baldy watershed — to percolate into the alluvial soils.

We can mimic this low-cost, low-energy, natural-system approach to water management, as Orange County has done in its massive stormwater capture and recharge operation. At a smaller scale, Pomona College, along with neighboring campuses at The Claremont Colleges, has built green infrastructure to increase the amount of pervious surface and divert rushing water into bioswales that filter out toxins and slowly regenerate the water beneath our feet.

Will they work? Amid the punishing drought of the mid-2010s, some of my students decided to find out by conducting a semester-long scientific analysis of the Pomona College system. Day after day of cloudless skies frustrated their plans. Even though minuscule amounts of precipitation were predicted for one night or another, they woke up in the pre-dawn hours, set up their instruments, and waited. As precise as these tools are, they did not register light mist. Pivoting, the team commandeered hoses, flushed a thin stream of water from various points at the apex of the streetscape in hopes of replicating the path that rain might take to enter the campus bioswales. Even as they figured out the watershed's size and extent, something that the architects of the bioswales did not know, they learned, as we all did, that sometimes nature does not cooperate with our best laid plans.

That cautionary tale comes with another: Punching holes in our paved-over landscape will not resolve all this region's water needs. That said, doing so will help reinforce the idea that we live in watersheds, a heightened consciousness that must be ingrained if we hope to build a more resilient future.

Restoring Big Tujunga

Students from John Marshall High School in Los Angeles received a hands-on lesson in just how tough watershed restoration can be. In 2013, as part of a larger project to restore the fire-and-flood battered Big Tujunga Canyon, located in the Angeles National Forest, they boarded buses, left their Los Feliz campus, and headed for the nearby Interstate 5 where it parallels the Los Angeles River in the Glendale Narrows. That geographical connection was important: their hour-long ride followed the river's path north and when the bus exited for the canyon, the students encountered one of the river's key high-ground tributaries. It's also the site of one of its post-fire dilemmas: invasive smilo grass, which resembles rice plants, had rapidly rooted in the burned-over landscape. Among their activities that day was pulling up the hardy plant, which has been making in-roads in disturbed canyons and watersheds across Southern California. The work was hot, hard, and dirty, a sweaty initiation into the challenges that ecosystems — and those who would try to restore them — daily face.

Their field trip underscored as well that this forest, like those across the country, have become increasingly vulnerable to the cumulative consequences of past management practices, catastrophic disturbances, and a warming climate. To restore resiliency to imperiled terrain, the National Forest Foundation (NFF), which Congress designated in 1991 as the official non-profit partner of the US Forest Service, launched a campaign that identified places of greatest need. With a one-to-one matching contribution from the Forest Service, the NFF committed to raise millions of dollars to restore the identified lands.

One of the selected sites was the Angeles National Forest, which at a thousand square miles, nearly the land equivalent of Rhode Island, constitutes Southern California's biggest playground, accounting for more than seventy percent of open space in greater Los Angeles. As vital as the recreation opportunities it provides, this urban national forest, which covers much of the San Gabriel Mountains with its tall peaks and sharp-cut canyons, also captures much-needed precipitation blowing off the Pacific; perhaps one-third of the region's water supply drains off the Angeles.

By 2013 when the John Marshall contingent arrived in Big Tujunga canyon, this life-giving watershed clearly was in trouble, partially the consequence of the 2009 Station Fire. Ignited by an arsonist late that August, it blew up into the largest conflagration in the recorded history of Los Angeles. Torching approximately two hundred and fifty square miles during its two-month-long fiery run, it burned through chaparral shrubland, oak woodlands, and up-elevation mixed pine forests.

Particularly hard hit were riparian and terrestrial ecosystems along streams within the upper reaches of the Los Angeles River, including those in Big Tujunga Canyon. Depending on the location within the 97,000-acre canyon, the Station Fire charred upwards of ninety-five percent of the sub-watershed's vegetation.

As every Angeleno knows, or should understand, wildland fire comes with a one-two punch. After flames scorch the earth during the now-extended spring-to-fall fire season, the unstable soil can wash away in a hurry if lashed by winter storms. That pattern manifested during the colder, rainy months of late 2009 into early 2010. According to the NFF, the post-storm sediment discharge from Big Tujunga Canyon alone was estimated to be three to four times higher than normal, and the sediment that those waters carried increased to levels fifteen to twenty-five times higher than normal during the first post-fire year.

Those super-heavy debris-and-rock flows, with the battering force of concrete slurry, gouged out creek beds and riverbeds, rampaged through sensitive habitat, and damaged regional water quality, endangering aquatic species such as the Santa Ana speckled dace, arroyo chub, Santa Ana sucker, and the western pond turtle.

Some of the harm will be repaired through a slow process of natural regeneration, as has occurred over the millennia. But Los Angeles can't wait as it depends on this canyon for water. Its recreational offerings are also crucial—more than one million visitors annually walk its trails, camp, fish, or simply rest beneath the shade of a spreading oak. The biodiversity that it sustains is equally invaluable. For those reasons, the NFF, the Forest Service, and a host of local partners agreed to raise $5 million to accelerate the restoration of Big Tujunga.

This substantial sum, half of which will come from matching funds from the Forest Service, allows the partnership to tackle some critical projects. For example, most of the canyon's recreational structures, picnic areas, and other sites were destroyed or damaged in the fire. Funds to rebuild them and repair the battered trail system, as well as enhance the educational outreach possibilities inherent in this hands-on work, are key elements of the campaign.

Dollars were also targeted at restoring streams and creeks that were seriously degraded in the fire and post-fire floods, damage that compromises the ability of native aquatic and land-based species to recover to pre-fire numbers. Likewise, money is needed to regenerate the 43,000 acres of forestland that the Station Fire consumed, 11,000 of which are expected to convert to grassland without intervention.

The driving concern behind these restoration plans is on-the-ground evidence that invasive plants and animals have taken and will continue to take advantage of the fire's disruptive force, establishing a competitive advantage over native species. The invasive flora and fauna can alter the canyon's landscape in many negative ways and these impacts are likely to worsen with shifts in temperature and precipitation that climate change is generating.

Although not all these alterations can be countered or controlled, the fund supports the removal of noxious weed populations by hand, and by chemical and mechanical means. It also funds the replanting of native shrubs and trees of various ages to increase the landscape's resilience. This multi-layered project will also have profound downstream implications for the thirteen million people who live within a one-hour drive of the Angeles National Forest and who draw some of their potable water from its flow. Regenerating these upcountry watersheds, in short, is vital to the public's health and well-being.

Forging a link between upstream and downstream—a connectedness the students witnessed first-hand from their bus windows and on-the-ground experiences—is integral to the

NFF's ambition to rebuild the resiliency of local ecosystems, strengthen the communities that lie adjacent to them, and increase public support for the lands themselves and the many species that inhabit them.

Most compelling is the broad, encompassing, and collaborative character of this initiative, for it marks an important shift in policy. Until the 1980s, public-lands management was a top-down process; decisions were made with little public consultation or input. The Forest Service and other federal and state agencies were frequently criticized for stewarding these lands without accounting for alternative insights or traditional knowledge, which in turn led to grassroots protests and legal challenges in the courts.

Beginning with the National Environmental Policy Act (1970) and a series of other public-access initiatives that the federal courts have upheld, and driven by budgetary shortfalls that have hampered careful management of our national forests, the Forest Service has become increasingly open to private-sector partnerships and community engagement. The NFF has reinforced these efforts by supporting hundreds of community-based non-profits working with the Forest Service to enhance civil society.

To nurture these engagements on the Angeles National Forest, for example, the NFF deployed the Conservation Connect program. Designed to serve community-based groups and Forest Service employees committed to collaborative restoration, it offers peer learning, technical assistance and training, and the facilitation of cooperative endeavors. This strategy builds on some of the Forest Service's founding principles. In 1905, Forest Service chief Gifford Pinchot, argued that these remarkable forests and grasslands were "made for and owned by the people," an argument with significant policy implications. "If the National Forests are going to accomplish anything worthwhile," he asserted, "the people must know all about them and must take a very active role in their management."

The Marshall High students experienced just how active, active could be—one thick-rooted clump of smilo grass at a time. Yet they also gained an enlarged perspective of their place in this larger watershed, the ineluctable connection between the Big Tujunga Canyon and their home grounds, key features of Southern California's natural inheritance and cultural legacy.

Danger Below

What if. That's the subtext of a field trip my students and I take to the San Antonio Canyon Dam. Built in the aftermath of the fatal 1938 flood and completed in 1956, the intimidatingly large earthen dam contains more than six million cubic yards of material, enough to build a twelve-foot-wide trail between New York City and Philadelphia. The dam's crest runs 3,850 feet across the canyon's mouth and soars one hundred sixty feet above its foundation. There is no better vantage point for understanding the relationship between the San Gabriel Mountains above and the Pomona Valley and Ontario Plain below.

To situate themselves in this site, I ask my students for a 360-degree evaluation of what they see: they may sketch, draw, photograph, or journal about this place before we discuss their evaluations. Inevitably they start with the canyon's steep slopes, some of which are a sheer eighty-percent grade, nearly vertical. They draw or reference the tight, twenty-seven-square-mile catchment area whose formidable apex is the 10,060-foot Mount Baldy. Then they shift to the dam itself and the channelized San Antonio Creek that runs southwesterly across the valley below, before converging with Chino Creek that carries its flow to Prado Dam to the south and east. But what really catches their eyes is the innumerable suburban subdivisions that abut the lower dam and crowd along the creek as far as the eye can see. This view is the crucial lesson in Southern California's urban geography that's replicated across the region's inland valleys and basins.

The dense built environment seems as inevitable and unmovable as the San Gabriel Mountains themselves. That's when I bring up the near disaster of the Oroville Dam, a stunning reminder that Californians live in a landscape of extremes. Nothing is as solid as it appears.

In late 2015, for example, the Oroville Reservoir was a poster child of the state's withering drought—fish carcasses littered its dust-cracked floor, marina docks ended in mid-air, a feeling of desolation haunted the emptied reservoir. Then snow and rain fell. Eighteen months later, there was so much water cascading over the dam's spillway that it cracked the main and emergency spillways, threatened the massive dam's structural integrity, and forced nearly two hundred thousand people to evacuate.

This rapid oscillation between drought and deluge was not a one-off. It's a harbinger of California's climate-changed environment. Over the rest of this century, scientists confirm, the Golden State will experience even more intense swings between dry and wet periods. If you thought Oroville was bad, just wait.

Only we cannot wait. Especially not in Southern California. For all our dependence on the water that Oroville and dams like it impound and then channel into the State Water Project, it is another kind of dam—those retaining floodwaters sheeting off the Santa Monica, San Gabriel, San Bernardino, and Santa Ana mountains—that has made it possible for development to sprawl across the inland valleys of this region.

These dams are as old, if not older, than Oroville. Their structural integrity is just as questionable. Which is why those built and operated by Los Angeles, San Bernardino, Riverside, and Orange counties are getting hurried-up inspections. Constructed in the aftermath of the Los Angeles River basin's massive 1938 flood, they were designed to withstand a similar fifty-year-storm event.

Yet the high-energy storms that will pound this region in subsequent decades will be much more powerful. Their power will morph into what researchers dub mega-floods. Should any of the local flood-retention dams collapse, the resulting devastation will be immense.

The US Army Corps of Engineers has made this case in its inspection reports of the dams it manages in Southern California. Among its key facilities are the Hanson and Sepulveda dams in San Fernando Valley—without which it would have been impossible to build the 101 and 5 freeways, and the packed-like-sardines suburbs that fan out from them. Other essential and vulnerable infrastructure include the Whittier Narrows Dam, which controls the San Gabriel River to protect the downstream communities of Montebello (Population: 61,000), Pico Rivera (ditto), Downey (110,000) and other cities clustered within the river's floodplain and abut its high-walled channels, all the way to Long Beach. The San Antonio Canyon Dam, which seals off the eponymous canyon above Ontario, Upland, Claremont and Pomona, is one of many such structures within the Santa Ana River watershed that are of considerable concern. Most central of them is the Prado Dam, which holds back all water in that river's upper watershed and defends several million residents of Orange County—including Mickey Mouse and the Happiest Place on Earth.

That each of these facilities needs repair is hardly good news. Hanson (built in 1940) and Sepulveda (1941) are in the best shape, but the Corps is concerned about their ability to withstand heavy flooding and earthquake deformation. The Whitter Narrows (1957) is the worst rated Corps-dam in the region, a high-hazard structure whose automatic spillway gates are antiquated; the foundation of this earthen structure "has a higher likelihood of failure" than previous understood and it may fail if overtopped.

The San Antonio Canyon Dam is only slightly more secure. Here, too, the Corps is worried about foundation seepage, possible collapse of channel walls and overtopping. "The likelihood of failure from one of these occurrences, prior to remediation," the Corps declared in 2008, "is too high to assure public safety." Remediation would cost $14 million, yet only $1 million has been allocated. The "urgent" safety issues of the dam remain unresolved.

Even more worrisome is Prado Dam. Since at least the 1980s, the *Los Angeles Times* has run scathing analyses of its deteriorating condition that conclude with urgent appeals for its immediate reconstruction. More recently, these tocsin editorials and fulminating opinion pieces have hammered three points about the dam built in 1940. Worried that climate-fueled flooding might undercut the current structure, the US Army Corps in 2019 elevated Prado Dam's risk category from moderate to high urgency. Its shaky status is even shakier, climate scientist Daniel Swain observed: "Federal engineers are finding that these systems are not as resilient as they thought they were, and that the frequency of what were regarded as once-in-a-lifetime storms is increasing significantly." Oh, and should the earth jolt at a high-enough magnitude, as it did during the 1971 and 1994 San Fernando earthquakes, then Prado and other local flood-retention structures that were constructed with outdated design and safety specifications, might well fail.

Given the crucial role Southern California's dams play in holding back floods, trapping sediment, and channeling water away from the thickly constructed built landscape that they were built to protect. Given that these downstream communities — their sprawling density and interlocking transportation grids — could not exist without flood-control infrastructure, their upgrading seems essential.

Undergirding that point are two of the class readings for the day of the field trip. The first is a sheaf of photographs of the 1938 flood's impact on Scripps and Pomona Colleges, which left the two campuses in a mud-choked disarray. The other: The City of Claremont's HazMat Plan, which indicates that should the dam collapse as a result of a mega-flood, debris-churned waters would reach the campuses and the downtown within twenty minutes. The documents hit home. Even though my students rightly pointed out that different policy decisions at another time might have produced a different result, they recognized the corresponding need to shore up the San Antonio Canyon Dam. As one put it as she boarded our bus home, "what a mess."

Desert Waters

When you think about potential new water sources for Southern California, the driest desert in North America, averaging only about five inches of precipitation per year, is not likely to be the first place that springs to mind. But the controversial Cadiz, Inc. water project has managed to keep that preposterous scenario afloat for decades.

Cadiz's dubious plan pumps sixteen billion gallons of groundwater each year, enough for around 160,000 households, from beneath Mojave Trails National Monument. The water would be sold to east San Gabriel Valley cities like Claremont, Pomona, La Verne and Covina — cities better off investing in water conservation and recycling to stretch their supplies.

It's a mess that involves a group of obscure public agencies located across the region. You might even get your tap water from one of them.

So far, publicly held Cadiz has evaded adequate environmental review of its project, funneling its state review through its lead customer, Orange County's Santa Margarita Water District. It also tried to take advantage of its connections in the Trump administration to sidestep federal oversight altogether — one of its former lawyers was Deputy Interior Secretary in that administration.

The company's political muscle has run into a scientific problem, however. Groundwater researchers have demonstrated that the Fenner Aquifer that Cadiz would mine is linked to several springs in the arid Mojave, particularly Bonanza Spring in the national monument. Suck up that groundwater, and those springs disappear, with disastrous effects on imperiled wildlife. Botanists have also demonstrated that damaging the springs will lead to the die off of any number of endangered or threatened plants.

In 2019, the state of California stepped up to make sure that the project's likely environmental impacts get a hard look from independent scientists. That year, state senator Richard Roth (D-Riverside) introduced SB 307, legislation requiring state agencies to assess the project and the damage it would cause to springs and desert wildlife.

Cadiz tried to deflect this scientific criticism and political challenges by claiming that its groundwater management plan actually would protect the environment once they start pumping. Environmental activists counter that Cadiz's plan is based on assumptions that geologists already have disproven.

To challenge this scientific data, Cadiz used Three Valleys Municipal Water District in eastern Los Angeles County and the Jurupa Community Services District in Riverside County to co-sponsor what they have called a "peer review" of its groundwater plan, written by four consultants.

That report was released at a special meeting of the Three Valleys board in March 2019. Unsurprisingly, those Cadiz-sponsored "experts" concluded that Cadiz's project would not hurt the desert. Embarrassingly for Three Valleys, critics revealed at that meeting that three of the four authors were longtime Cadiz supporters, and the whole project was paid for by Cadiz with the money funneled through an intermediary.

The so-called "independent peer review" of the Cadiz plan, in other words, was neither independent nor a peer review. It was yet another corporate-sponsored PR campaign masquerading as objective science.

Instead of providing a real fact-check of Cadiz's claims, it's a shame the Three Valleys MWD decided to prop up Cadiz's increasingly discredited project. Despite this, Three Valleys' gaffe is a stark reminder of the importance of having truly independent scientists examine all such water schemes in California.

Because of this debacle, California lawmakers redoubled their efforts to pass SB 307 to stop the Cadiz project. As the legislation's proponents noted in the spring of 2019, the bill would free Three Valleys to focus on adopting water-conservation technologies and strategies that will create a more resilient region as it warms up and dries out.

Unquenchable Thirst

California's water legislation, SB307, designed to stop Cadiz from pumping desert groundwater, may prove to be far-reaching in its consequences. Governor Gavin Newsom signed the bill into law on July 31, 2019 requiring independent review from the State Lands Commission, Department of Fish and Wildlife and the Department of Water Resources to ensure that pumping from the groundwater basin does not harm the natural or cultural resources at the site and in the surrounding watersheds.

Focused on short-term impact, a columnist at the *Desert Sun,* decried the bill as a job-killer and legislative overreach. The *Los Angeles Times* and the *Sacramento Bee* read the law as another Golden State rebuke of the Trump administration due to its support for the Cadiz project, and these newspapers made much of the legislation's protection of imperiled Mojave Desert springs and species. The environmental impact of the law was a point that Senator Dianne Feinstein confirmed: "If Cadiz were allowed to drain a vital desert aquifer, everything that makes our desert special — from bighorn sheep and desert tortoises to Joshua trees and breathtaking wildflower blooms — would have been endangered."

These are all important considerations to be sure. But the new law is actually more expansive in reality and reach. Although the enduring battle over the control and distribution of water dates back to the Spanish conquest of Alta California in the late eighteenth century, SB 307 offers an important twist in the state's longstanding struggle to secure a sustainable supply of this essential resource.

In this case, the play for desert groundwater is a shock, not least because ever since the Gold Rush Sierran snowmelt has dominated the state's mirage-like fantasies of an unending stream of water that would blast open mineral riches, fill reservoirs, irrigate farms and lawns, drive industrial production, and wash windows, cars, and sidewalks. This natural tap would forever boom the state's economy. But could the desert, specifically the Mojave Desert, one of the most arid regions on this blue planet, also become a rich repository of water? That seems a contradiction in terms.

Adding to the confusion is that the main actors in this most-recent drama are not the usual suspects. This story is not about water grabs devised by Big Ag in the Central Valley. It is not about a scheming Metropolitan Water District, Southern California's dominant wholesaler of water to the region's many water-distribution agencies. Neither the City of Los Angeles nor the State of California, each of which in the past has diverted vast amounts of other regions' water for its own ends and ticked off a lot of people in the process, are the creators of this particular narrative.

Taking center stage instead is a clutch of venture capitalists who have invested in the Cadiz Project, and whose investment has underwritten the purchase of thirty-four thousand desert acres and associated water rights in San Bernardino County. Theirs is a supply-side operation, a tantalizing pool of water that has not yet been integrated into

California's highly complex water resource market. Should it ever be so—and despite SB 307, Cadiz will do everything in its power to make that happen—then privately owned groundwater will become a cash cow for Wall Street profiteers.

Standing in their way is this new law, which unflinchingly asks why are we still fixated on securing new supplies of hitherto unexploited water, by hook or by crook? Cadiz, after all, is one more shimmering proposal, in a long line of such illusions, that ever-dry Southern California can solve its water crises by pumping out the Owens River Valley, the Colorado River, or that trio of NorCal rivers, the Feather, Sacramento, or the San Joaquin. Absent this law, and the Mojave would be yet another victim of our unquenchable thirst.

The adoption of this law sheds light on a new approach to water management: the smartest, least expensive, and most efficient method of building a more water-resilient state is to tackle the demand side of the equation. This insight is at the heart of a 2018 argument by Peter Gleick, president Emeritus of the Pacific Institute, which appeared in the *Proceedings of the National Academy of Sciences.* He dubs the new water-management paradigm the "soft water path," which refocuses on the "multiple benefits water provides, improving water use efficiency, integrating new technology for decentralized water sources, modernizing management systems, committing to ecological restoration, and adopting more effective economic approaches." By rigorous conservation we can do more with less.

That prospect is not new. The implementation and constant improvement of low-flow technologies are required features in building codes across California. It was strikingly manifest, amid a punishing four-year drought, in the rapid decrease in urban water use following Governor Jerry Brown's April 2015 declaration of mandatory emergency restrictions to cut consumption by twenty-five percent. It's evident as well in Orange County's highly successful groundwater replenishment operation—to date, the world's largest—that captures and treats stormwater and effluent to the EPA's highest standard for potable water. The project currently serves more than 850,000 consumers.

This replenishment system is making a critical contribution to the county's ambition to become water independent by 2050, an ambition that the UCLA Institute of the Environment and Sustainability believes Los Angeles County could replicate. In its 2018 report, the center highlighted "potential pathways to a transformation of the city's historical reliance on imported water to an integrated, green infrastructure, water management approach that provides water quality, supply, flood control, habitat, open space and other benefits."

Galvanizing policymakers, politicians, and taxpayers to invest in these proven, real-world outcomes will not be easy. UCLA researchers, however, believe that the impact of recent and punishing droughts have had on "water supplies throughout California has created a new urgency to increase the city's ability to provide a secure, resilient water supply through local sources." SB307 might accelerate that transition by helping break our bad habit of relying on Cadiz-like pipe dreams, which the late historian Norris Hundley argues in *The Great Thirst: Californians and Water* was "born of an earlier era when abundance encouraged abuse." If it does so, then it will mark a significant turning point in the state's contentious water history.

Follow the Money

In California's water politics, it always pays to follow the money. So advised UCLA historian Norris Hundley, author of *The Great Thirst: Californians and Water* (2001). After all, the unfettered pursuit of water in this state, so precious a resource that some have called it white gold, has prompted the rise of a "new kind of social imperialist whose goal was to acquire the water of others and prosper at their expense, a goal that catapulted California into a modern colossus while also producing monumental conflicts and social costs."

A small but significant example of Hundley's assessment of the enduring conflicts and costs is the $805,000 grant that Cadiz, Inc., a well-funded water-mining project in the Mojave Desert, in early 2020 gave to Three Valleys Municipal Water District, headquartered in Claremont. That grant amounts to a dollar for each person that Three Valleys serves in Claremont and several other jurisdictions in eastern Los Angeles County. The money will not be distributed to the ratepayers. It won't underwrite badly needed water conservation initiatives. Instead, the payoff is a different kind, which is why following its paper trail is as crucial as revelatory.

Southern California is home to dozens of local water districts that usually fly well beneath the radar. Their actions usually only rise to the surface when, for example, their directors get caught with their hands in the till or fail to provide clean, safe water. One such problem child is the Central Basin Municipal Water District, a public agency, which provides water to the three separate and private water purveyors in Maywood. A target of an FBI corruption investigation in 2013, CBMWD also has been accused of providing substandard water. "It's kind of brown, almost like tea, and it tastes like rotten eggs," one resident complained.

Whatever their level of conscientiousness, individual and localized agencies collectively have a region-wide impact on Southern California's water future. That has been particularly apparent during the seven-year drought that began in 2010. It served as a dramatic wakeup call for officials at all levels of government, as well as water purveyors and residents. Nearly everyone recognized that the region needed to institute rigorous conservation measures. Governor Jerry Brown was among many arguing that slowing consumption was the least expensive and most effective way to ratchet down demand for costly imported water that flowed into Southern California via the Los Angeles Aqueduct, State Water Project, and Colorado River Aqueduct.

In contrast to the unanimity of opinion about conservation, and the subsequent measures that demonstrated its effectiveness, the Cadiz grant to Three Valleys has been designed to force continued reliance on expensive, imported water via long-distance infrastructure. If successful, this scheme will erode the last decade's commitments to the three Rs of water conservation: reduce, reuse and recycle.

Cadiz's plan to pump and sell desert groundwater makes this clear. One of the agencies transfixed by the Cadiz mirage is Three Valleys Municipal Water District. In late February, it accepted that bundle of Cadiz cash to underwrite "independent research" of the Mojave project's environmental impact.

Actually, the grant is a pass-through. Three Valleys handed it off to the consulting firm Aquilogics. There's little reason to believe its research and results will be truly independent. Consider, for example that Anthony Brown, who heads Aqualogics, already has written numerous newspaper commentaries advocating for the Cadiz project and arguing that its pumping scheme will not damage ecosystems. "Now is not the time to be playing policy games to stop environmentally reviewed projects," he wrote in 2015. "Now more than ever is the time for the Cadiz Water Project to finally proceed."

Like Brown, Three Valleys has a vested interest in this research's predetermined outcome. In 2010, the district signed an option agreement to procure Cadiz's water. The not-so-hidden agenda of the Cadiz-Three Valleys-Aquilogics study preordains the conclusion that the project is environmentally benign and sustainable. Cadiz is gambling that that salutary result will improve the project's odds of passing muster with an upcoming mandatory review by the California State Lands Commission that SB 307 requires.

The odds of approval are not in Cadiz's favor, as peer-reviewed scholarship has documented the potential project's deleterious impact. As independent researchers Adam H. Love and Andy Zdon note in a recent paper in *Hydrology* (2018), and in another co-authored article in *Environmental Forensics* (2018), pumping large volumes of Mojave groundwater will significantly lower the regional water table and its many interconnected springs. If that occurs, their scientific analyses reveal, these desert springs will disappear and endanger the flora and fauna that inhabit these arid lands, among the driest in the nation.

Governor Newsom noted in August 2019 while signing SB 307: "Water has flowed underneath the Mojave for thousands of years, sustaining the Native Americans, bighorn sheep, the threatened desert tortoise and a variety of other plant and animal life that have made the Mojave Desert their home."

Protecting the endangered Mojave is essential. So is prioritizing strict water conservation. Both will make the region more sustainable, habitable, and resilient. Whether Cadiz, Inc. can fulfill these vital environmental goals and convince the California Lands Commission that its project will do no harm is the $805,000 question.

SAFE HAVENS

This Land is Their Land

However polite its title, the 1891 "Petition to the Senators and Representatives of the Congress of the United States in the Behalf of the Remnants of the former Tribes of the Yosemite Indians Praying for Aid and Assistance" was anything but deferential.

The petition offered a blunt critique of the mostly white gold miners' brutal incursion into the Yosemite region in the late 1840s. It sharply criticized the state-sanctioned violence that California unleashed in the 1850s on the Indigenous Peoples of the Central Sierra, and astutely recognized that elite tourists—and the amenities they required to cushion their late nineteenth-century visits to the rugged landscape—were also responsible for cultural disruption and physical dispossession. The petition reported that the previous half century of exploitation had turned the Ahwahneechee and Mono into "poorly-clad paupers and unwelcome guests, silently the objects of curiosity or contemptuous pity to the throngs of strangers who yearly gather in this our own land and heritage."

The once fertile and sustaining terrain of the Indigenous Peoples had been torn apart. "The gradual destruction of its trees, the occupancy of every foot of its territory by bands of grazing horses and cattle, the decimation of the fish in the river, the destruction of every means of support for ourselves and families by the rapacious acts of the whites," the petition asserted, would "shortly result in the total exclusion of the remaining remnants of our tribes from this our beloved valley, which has been ours from time beyond our faintest traditions, and which we still claim."

The US government did not respond to this appeal for the return of tribal lands, an ironclad treaty that would protect their inheritance, and compensation for their decades of immiseration. Instead, the petition, to which forty-three survivors put their names, was buried in the 1891 report of Yosemite's acting park superintendent. But its bureaucratic fate doesn't diminish its importance any more than does the probability that the document's amanuensis was a Euro-American fluent in English. The oral histories on which the petition depends, and, as anthropologist Ed Castillo observed, the "incredible description" it provides of the "political, military, and ecological factors driving remaining tribesmen from their valley could only have as their source local Indigenous knowledge."

That knowledge, and the distressing catalogue of injustices it contains, is an important challenge to settler-colonial justifications for How the West Was Won. One facet of that master narrative also centers on Yosemite National Park—by the time tourists arrived to "ooh and ahhh" over its iconic waterfalls, steep granite walls, and staggering vistas, the land was "empty." Its putative emptiness, the result of violent dispossession, set the stage for an early twentieth-century, decade-long battle over whether to build a dam in the park's Hetch Hetchy Valley. The dam's proponents, including federal officials, as well as citizens and politicians in

San Francisco eager to secure a stable water supply following the 1906 earthquake that devastated the city, believed the dam was emblematic of Progressive Era reforms that provided essential—and publicly owned—resources to a rapidly urbanizing society. John Muir, founding president of the Sierra Club, which was established in 1892, was among those who pushed back, arguing that the dam's construction would inundate the wild Hetch Hetchy Valley. "Dam Hetch Hetchy!" he thundered, "as well dam for water-tanks the people's cathedrals and churches, for no holier temple has ever been consecrated for the heart of man."

What neither side admitted was that their respective arguments depended on a shared perception that no one lived in the Hetch Hetchy Valley, or that no had ever lived there. Its emptiness enabled dam supporters to conclude that the site would be perfect for a reservoir. Its emptiness, for those like Muir who pressed for the valley's preservation, was a mark of its higher utility as pristine nature. Yet to conceive of this valley as devoid of people required two forms of erasure of the history and contemporary status of the Indigenous Peoples that their 1891 petition so brilliantly evoked.

The first erasure occurred in the mid-nineteenth century, when California and the United States governments sanctioned the violent expulsion of the Indigenous Peoples from the Sierra's flanking valleys and foothills. The dispossession of the Miwok, Paiute, Shoshone, and others from their ancestral territories was an act of genocide, historian Benjamin Madley argues in *American Genocide*. He writes: the "pressures of demographics (the migration of hundreds of thousands of immigrants), economics (the largest gold rush in US history), and profound racial hatred all made the genocide possible, it took sustained political will—at both the federal and state levels—to create the laws, policies, and well-funded killing machine that carried it out and ensured its continuation over decades."

The second erasure is embedded in the continuing and disquieting silence over the interlocking connection between the ruthless uprooting of Indigenous Peoples from the Yosemite region, the establishment of the national park, and the subsequent Hetch Hetchy controversy. Until that silence is broken, our understanding of the ongoing debate about the dam and reservoir will remain incomplete. This accounting is especially necessary because scholars and activists assert that the formative battle over the Hetch Hetchy dam marked the birth of the modern environmental movement in the United States. The assertion reveals a troubling and complicated story.

Muir was integral to each of these erasures. Consider his reflections that he jotted down in his journal after a hike up what he called Bloody Canyon in Mono County and then revised for publication in his book The *Mountains of California* (1894). Entering the pass, the "huge rocks began to close around in all their wild, mysterious impressiveness," Muir wrote, "when suddenly, as I gazed eagerly about me, a drove of gray, hairy beings came into sight, lumbering toward with a kind of boneless, wallowing motion like bears." Anxious about "so grim a company," and suppressing his fears, he realized "that although hairy as bears and as crooked as summit pines, the strange creatures were sufficiently erect to belong to our own species." He was hiking up a trail that the Mono and other Indigenous Peoples had worn smooth over the millennia, transiting between the Mono and Owens basins and Yosemite and the valleys below. His disdain for these men and women shows throughout his descriptions, such as, "the dirt on their faces was fairly stratified and seemed so ancient and so undisturbed it might almost possess a geological significance." To Muir they belonged to a distant time, and befouled his wilderness. "Somehow they seemed to have no right place in the landscape, and I was glad to see them fading out of sight down the pass."

The larger settler-colonial culture adopted his perspective and, whether Indigenous Peoples were forced out of Yosemite by force of arms or the scratch of a pen, a key consequence was that this "empty" terrain was ripe for commercial exploitation. Tourism to the region, enabled by a growing cross-continental transportation grid, and the growth of San Francisco and Los Angeles, was fueled by artists and photographers who visited the region a decade or more before Muir's arrival there in 1868. James Mason Hutchings, who hired Muir to work at his Yosemite hotel, was a relentless promoter. He drew a swelling number of artists, scientists, and tourists to make the arduous journey to the remote location through his publication of tour guides, lithographs, and magazine articles about Yosemite's wonders and curiosities. Many of these visitors recounted their experiences in the rough and wild space, some published, others not. However manifest, these documents reinforced the cultural conversation about what they perceived to be Yosemite's prime value—a beneficent refuge in an industrializing world, where you could escape civilization, and yet have its amenities.

The sanctuary status was one of the key arguments that Muir and others developed in the early twentieth century against the city of San Francisco and its political allies who laid claim to the Hetch Hetchy Valley inside what became Yosemite National Park. The thrust and counterthrust manifested in a series of congressional hearings, in the pages of many of the nation's leading magazines and newspapers, and in oft angry speeches. The fierce debate testifies to the centrality of a valley that few Americans had ever visited. Even though San Francisco's interests prevailed, and the O'Shaughnessy Dam and its steep-walled reservoir that funnels potable water to the Bay Area was built, the controversy continues to simmer. Beginning in the 1980s, an odd coalition of Republican state and national politicians and the Sierra Club and its allies periodically call into question San Francisco's reliance on the reservoir and urge the federal government to tear down the dam and restore the long-submerged valley.

Yet any resolution of this latest struggle to determine the future of Hetch Hetchy, and by extension Yosemite, must start by prioritizing what hitherto has been ignored. Novelist, historian, and activist David Treuer writes, "America's national parks comprise only a small fraction of the land stolen from Native Americans, but they loom large in the broader story of our dispossession." His pithy conclusion — "the American West began with war but concluded with parks" — is mirrored in the Yosemite Indigenous Peoples' claims asserted in the 1891 petition: "We say this valley was not given to us by our fathers for a day, or a year, but for all time."

Coastal Haze

John Riis, a young forest ranger, first encountered the Santa Barbara National Forest (now Los Padres) in the early twentieth century. In his memoir, *Ranger Trails*, he waxed lyrically, "Sometimes we rode down lanes of flaming pepper trees, or reached up to pluck an orange or an English walnut from an overhanging bough." This place of plenty boggled his imagination. "There were long evenings on the strand; moonlit evenings when the smell of orange blossoms mingled with the salt tang of the sea and the sleepy surges of the Pacific whispered mysterious tales of the Orient to the white sands on the beach." Having transferred from the La Sal reserve in "the dry deserts of Utah," Santa Barbara "was like being dropped at the gates of Paradise."

Another who wrote penetratingly, definitively of this Edenic land was Robinson Jeffers, the poet laureate of California's rough central coast. "The shining ocean below lay on the Shore," he observed in *Cawdor*, "Like the great shield of the moon come down, rolling bright rim/to rim with the earth. Against it the multiform/And many-canyoned coast-range hills were gathered into one/carven mountain." As Jeffers brought this terrain to life—green hills studded with oak and pine that seem to pitch into the Pacific, white waves crashing against black rock—he warned that "No imaginable/Human presence here could do anything/But dilute the lonely self-watchful passion."

Jeffers, like Riis, would be shocked by how some humans have trampled this staggering beauty, despoiling what has made the 1.75 million-acre Los Padres National Forest so attractive to so many visitors. Follow then not the poet's gaze seaward but toward the narrow trails east, snaking up creek, ravine, and canyon into the Coastal and Transverse ranges. In winter, figures move up remote, fog-wrapped paths seeking relatively flat ground with access to a thin trickle or rush of water. They dump their bulky backpacks, weighed down with tools, food, poisonous chemicals, plastic piping, and tents, and begin cutting trees and clearing the ground, manually and with herbicides. Then they set to work laying out waterlines, building check dams, and digging into the soil before planting thousands of cannabis seeds.

Within weeks, marijuana is growing quickly in the warm California sun, fed with diverted stream flow and fertilizers, and protected from predators by the thick application of rodenticides and other toxicants. The drug cartels running illegal grows have been targeting the US public lands generally, and in particular the Golden State's twenty million acres of national forests and doing so with devastating effect. "Marijuana growing on public lands has been going on for 30 plus years, but they have just expanded dramatically," observes Daryl Rush, a special agent in the Forest Service's Law Enforcement and Investigations unit. "Every forest is impacted and the majority of our workload is on marijuana investigations on the forest."

Among those most battered is Los Padres. In 2013 alone, officers discovered forty-seven trespass grows (as they are called), uprooted

181,139 marijuana plants (the most ever in the state), and removed the following:

    Infrastructure—19,710 pounds
    Restricted poisons—138 ounces
    Fertilizer—4,595 pounds
    Common pesticides—12 gallons
    Waterline—29,599 feet (5.6 miles)
    20-pound propane bottles—48
    16-ounce propane bottles—54
    Car batteries—7
    Dams and reservoirs—12

That same summer, strike forces were active on the Cleveland National Forest (nine grows yielding over sixteen thousand plants), the Angeles (twenty-seven sites budding with over seventy-six thousand plants), and the San Bernardino (where they destroyed nearly one hundred fifteen thousand plants on twenty-one sites). Other hard-hit forests included the Sequoia, Shasta-Trinity, Sierra, and Plumas, averaging over one hundred ten thousand plants each.

The reality in these forests is much worse than the data suggests. Given the difficulty in detecting these illegal sites, hidden by tree canopies and only accessible by climbing into a rugged backcountry, officers can make but a small dent in growing operations statewide. Indeed, in 2012 the Forest Service reported that more than eighty-three percent of the over one million plants eradicated from National Forests were eradicated in California, making it the national epicenter.

All the canisters, boxes, bags, and bottles of pesticides, herbicides, and rodenticides—a wickedly toxic brew that Rachel Carson decried as "elixirs of death"—poisons the soil and works its way into the terrestrial, riparian, and marine biota.

Consider what has happened to the Pacific fisher. Despite its name, the furry and furtive mammal does not live in or near the coast but instead occupies the same remote, closed-canopy forests that growers are degrading, among them the Los Padres. UC-Berkeley's Sierra Nevada Adaptive Management Project autopsied fisher carcasses from northern and central California and determined that nearly eighty percent were poisoned by anticoagulants, the source of which is undoubtedly marijuana plantations.

Compounding the fisher's vulnerability is the interwoven nature of its diet, which consists of small mammals, birds, and fruit, and which contributes to its intake of toxicants. That same is true for the prey of eagles, owls, vultures, mountain lions, and foxes. The Los Padres, among other beautiful national forests, and the critical biodiversity they sustain, are becoming lethal.

Well-armed trespass growers also threaten hikers and rangers. The number of weapons confiscated from the sites, including high-powered assault rifles, along with anecdotes of gun-toting "farmers" menacing hikers who stumble on their grows, has spiked in recent years. This dangerous situation is creating a chill factor, limiting people's access to the Great Outdoors, to the splendid recreational opportunities these national forests offer to millions of Californians.

Increased safety will never be fully achieved by the important, if ad hoc, campaign to root out illegal marijuana grows. There are too many of these sites, and they are too difficult to locate, to insure their complete eradication. Besides, the demand for marijuana, and the cash to be made is so great that cartels have little incentive to alter their business model. It's unlikely that they will be deterred by the well-intentioned decision the US Sentencing Commission reached in 2014 to strengthen sentencing guidelines and include environmental damage for those caught on trespass grows.

Combating the growers' brutal impact on watersheds, hillsides, and woodlands requires a massive infusion of fiscal and human resources, or a political solution of legalization and regulation like those in Colorado, Washington, and California. Whatever decisions voters and policymakers reach, one of their goals must be the protection and restoration of the complex biodiversity, manifold recreational opportunities, and legitimate economic operations in national forests and public lands affected by trespass grows. By enabling these compromised lands to spring back to life we would also fulfill Robinson Jeffers' moral imperative: "It is time for us to kiss the earth again."

Unsanctified

One confounding Obama-era national monument is the Basin and Range, a seven hundred thousand-acre wind-swept, high desert site in southeastern Nevada. It's not puzzling because the designation protects "one of the most undisturbed corners of the broader Great Basin region, which extends from the Sierra Nevada Mountains in the west to the Colorado Plateau in the east," an unusual pattern of "basin, fault, and range that ... creates a dramatic topography that has inspired inhabitants for thousands of years." If you have ever flown over the area, it offers a striking vista. Nor is it puzzling that these federal lands, already managed by the Bureau of Land Management and which will continue to supervise them, contain Indigenous Peoples' sacred and cultural sites dating back thirteen thousand years, nor that it's home to a rich biota, from alpine heights to desert floor. And it was just as predictable that Republicans denounced the designation as a "federal land grab," despite most of the acreage was already federally owned.

There was a notable exception to federal ownership, and therein lies my confoundment. The Basin and Range National Monument envelops artist Michael Heizer's as-yet completed project known as "City," which he began to construct in 1972 on privately owned land in Garden Valley about three hours northwest of Las Vegas. Noting that the project is "one of the most ambitious examples of the distinctively American land art movement," the Obama proclamation identifies its monumentality as the key to its significance.

Built into and out of the vast undeveloped expanse of Garden Valley, the work combines modern abstract architecture and engineering with ancient American aesthetic influences on a monumental scale, roughly the size of the National Mall, and evokes the architectural forms of ancient Mesoamerican ceremonial cities like Teotihuacán and Chichén Itzá. The presence of City in this stark and silent landscape provides the visitor a distinctive lens through which to experience and interact with Garden Valley.

Here is where I balk. At more than a mile long and a quarter-mile wide, with its abstract, monolithic structures said to resemble ancient urbanisms, and its reconfigured and hardened spaces of rock and concrete, "City" has profoundly altered the terrain and thoroughly damaged the biodiverse habitats that this portion of Garden Valley once sustained. What makes its gashes and its staggering price tag which may soar to $25 million, any less disturbing than, say, Las Vegas? Has not each spatial slashing, each architectonic design feature, so thoroughly converted the desert into a built environment that it mocks the national monument's protective purposes? That question will be even more relevant when, or if, "City" is ever completed and becomes a formal part of the monument.

Okay. I confess that I'm not enthusiastic about either the land-art movement and Heizer's work particularly. His work first got under my skin in the fall of 2011 amid a gnawing recession, when well-heeled art patrons and donors kicked in more than $10 million to underwrite Heizer's earth-moving project, dubbed "Levitated Mass." It was installed at the Los Angeles County Museum of Art as a permanent, outdoor display.

The installation's name tells part of the story. Heizer suspended a massive 340-ton quartz boulder, the weight of a fully loaded jetliner, over a concrete slot four hundred fifty feet long, and fifteen feet deep. Its gargantuan size makes "massive" an understatement, which is also the artist's point. To construct something so large as to defy the imagination, so large that it took eight days to haul this very heavy load from the Stone Valley Quarry in Riverside, California to its destination more than fifty miles away in downtown Los Angeles, pushes (crushes may be a better term) the boundaries of what is thought possible. A minimalist Heizer has never been.

Yet his maximalist impulse is paired with an imperial reach, a chest-thumping sense of conquest—nature, from which this imposing rock has been ripped, is manipulable, acted upon. Art is what Heizer can forge out of its raw materials, bending them to his will—or, in this case, hanging it in mid-air, a triumph of technology and engineering. Nature is held in suspension.

This has been the leitmotif of his career. A key player in a movement known as land or earth art, which grew out of the cultural tumult of the 1960s and 1970s, Heizer is among those for whom the grand gesture of manipulating vast earthen forms has served as a protest against the spatial constraints galleries and museums by definition impose. However big their walls, they remain walls; however open-aired their structures, they remain structures.

These artists, including James Turrell and Robert Smithson, rejected what they perceived to be the commodification of art, its market and consumption, its price. If you could construct something so colossal it could not be housed in the usual way or sold in the normal manner, well, you had beaten the system.

Of course, you also would have to pummel the very landscape as a way make your mark. In 1969, for instance, Heizer went to the eastern edge of the Mormon Mesa, not far from Overton, Nevada. He used earth-moving machines to dig two deep trenches, fifty feet deep and thirty feet wide, each roughly seven hundred fifty feet long, that jutted out from the landform's southern and northern flanks. The project is called "Double Negative," a title and construct that led one of its admirers to enthuse.

In keeping with the mission of modern art, *Double Negative* blurs the distinction between sculpture ("art") and normal objects such as rocks ("not art"), and encourages viewers to consider how the earth relates to art. The sheer size of *Double Negative* also invites contemplation of the scale of art, and the relation of the viewer the earth and to art itself. How does art change when it can't fit in a museum? How does one observe an artwork that's a quarter-mile long?

Those are all good questions. But so, too, are these: How do the abstract purposes of these trenches account for the reality of two hundred forty thousand tons of rock, gravel, and sand displaced in their construction? How exactly does this earth relate to that art? Did Mormon Mesa — spare, arid, clean — require gross human intrusion to be more artful, more complete? Heizer's sculpture gives new meaning to Double Negative.

"Levitated Mass" exposes these concerns about the environmental impact of his oeuvre, about their masculinized monumentality. True, the enormous boulder was blasted out of working quarry in the foothills of the Jurupa Mountains, hardly a pristine landscape. Yet its ultimate presentation at LACMA—trussed up, harnessed—only reinforces its decontextualized state, its uprootedness. With its geological referents obliterated, its integrity gone, the boulder has become a commodity whose sculptural value is that which Heizer grants it—levitation. Now a mass, no longer a rock.

Over the years, there has been "a backlash against the grandiosity and possibly destructive nature of these projects," Ann Landi writes in *ArtNews*. She then rationalizes that the bulk of earth artists' schemes, including City and Double Negative, was "underway or completed when environmental restraints were nonexistent and before the general consciousness about ecology had been raised."

She gives Heizer and others too much cover. From Mary Austin's *Land of Little Rain* (1903) to Edward Abbey's *Desert Solitaire* (1968), American environmental culture has been infused with a compelling appreciation for the desert's raw power, its essential quiet and peaceful solitude, its dark skies. Its stunning otherness. These literary perceptions have found material expression in the establishment of three large desert parks in California in the early twentieth century: Death Valley National Park (1933), Joshua Tree National Park (1933), and Anza Borrego State Park (1933). Heizer, for one, was well aware of this encompassing tradition, once confiding that in "the desert, I can find that kind of unraped, peaceful, religious space artists have always tried to put in their work." I know, the irony in his words is chilling.

But Landi is correct in that one of the most troubling aspects of Heizer's work is its hubristic, anachronistic impulse. In the early twenty-first century, a new generation of environmental artists carry none of the Great White Man's Burden that Heizer and his peers hoisted onto their shoulders more than four decades ago. Instead, figures such as Alexsandra Mir and Andy Goldsworthy have been creating artworks made of found objects in nature, humble in scale, fragile and ephemeral.

Had he really wanted to shock the art world, Heizer might have adopted their more modest affect. We are told, for example, that he sketched out the idea for "Levitated Mass" in 1968, and spent the succeeding years seeking the perfect boulder. Once located in that dust-choked wash in Riverside County, he would have startled us all had he simply, softly walked away, his project complete.

Marine Life

Sir Francis Drake did not know from NOAA.

The marauding, wind-powered explorer of the California coast would have been startled to learn that the world has evolved to such an extent that nation states boast of institutions like the National Oceanic and Atmospheric Administration that regulate the bounding main and its rich waters. But like the federal agency, Drake knew full well how fecund the Pacific is.

On July 24, 1579, one day after he and the crew of the Golden Hind sailed from what Drake dubbed Nova Albion, now known as Drake's Bay, they dropped anchor at the Farallones, a small cluster of guano-encrusted islands and sea stacks off San Francisco Bay. What drew them to these stormed-tossed isles was food, "hauing on them plentifull and great store of Seales and birds … whereon we found such prouision as might competently serue our turne for a while."

Spelling aside, Drake's early record of the islands' teeming life, its profusion, is precisely why it's so important that NOAA announced in mid-2015 it was considerably expanding the Gulf of the Farallones National Marine Sanctuary and the adjacent Cordell Bank National Marine Sanctuary. The size of the expansion is breathtaking. The Farallones sanctuary, which had encompassed a substantial 1,282 square miles, swelled to 3,295 square miles. No wonder it later added the word "Greater" to the Farallones sanctuary). Also, the Cordell Bank sanctuary more than doubled in size, from 529 to 1,286 square miles. When combined with the Monterey National Marine Sanctuary to the south, NOAA now oversees a contiguous stretch of three hundred fifty miles of the California coast, more than a third of its entire length. Size matters.

Its new expansiveness is significant, too, because it means greater protection from the high tide mark in coves, rivers, estuaries to sixty miles out to sea. Among those species and sites benefiting from these increased protections are the rock and island haul-out spots for sea lions and elephant seals, which, as Drake discovered, also double as roosting and breeding zones for pelagic seabirds which live on open seas, including gulls, murres, and auklets. Sharks are in this mix as well, with new and larger "Great White Shark Approach Prohibition Areas."

One key reason why all those animals — threatened, endangered, and flourishing — make such extensive use of this protected marinescape is "the nutrient rich upwelling zone originating off Point Arena and flowing south into the original sanctuaries." Those nutrients make the sanctuary a "hotspot for wildlife" because, according to my colleague, Pomona College biologist Nina Karnovsky, they lead "to phytoplankton growth and then zooplankton grazers (basically 'crustacean cows') that become food for fish and seabirds and marine mammals." Nina, who with a gaggle of students has been studying the region for years observed, "Warming the California current has caused a decline in zooplankton so anything that helps the area stay healthy is good news." Put another way, by absorbing these currents and such subsea features as Bodega Canyon, the sanctuaries now are more ecosystemic in design.

They are no less human-centered in their expansive sweep. These surging, rough waters have claimed their share of shipwrecks dating back to the nineteenth century, and earlier. Airplanes that crashed into the waters are also to be found. So that scholars might locate, assess, and analyze these various historic and cultural artifacts, and feed the "keen public interest," the sanctuaries' designations expressly prohibit removing or damaging any artifacts.

Equally significant is the regulatory prohibition against dumping ballast, fuel, waste, and other effluent that shippers once routinely jettisoned into the ocean. This covers commercial vessels, cruise liners, and military ships that ply these waters—not an incidental number given that the Farallones sanctuary covers the central and northern approaches to San Francisco Bay, one of the nation's major shipping hubs.

These changes did not happen in a vacuum. In this case, a Democratic dynamo set these wheels in motion. Former US House Representative Lynn Woolsey, whose district included the California North Coast, began working on this project in the early twenty-first century with a coalition of fishing groups, environmental organizations, and local officials. She recognized that expanding the two sanctuaries would increase their ability to keep this portion of the white-capped Pacific resilient and vital—qualities that describe Woolsey herself. Her successor, Representative Jared Huffman, and congressional colleagues Sam

Farr, Lois Capps, Mike Thompson, and Jackie Speier cheered NOAA's new protections which have become part of Woolsey's conservation legacy.

Woolsey's legacy is contributing to the rewilding of the ocean and a regeneration of its biological integrity that over four hundred years ago so captivated—and nourished—an English captain and his crew.

Grand Design

In August 2016, President Obama went big. With a stroke of his pen, he quadrupled the area of the Papahānaumokuākea Marine National Monument in the center of the Pacific Ocean, northwest of Hawai'i. Whatever other conservation actions he took in his final months in office, Papahānaumokuākea was hard to top.

The new monument is also outsized in the interrelated issues it seeks to address — and may well generate. In Papahānaumokuākea, biology, politics and policy converge and collide in revelatory ways. And while it's clear the creation of this gigantic marine monument was a huge step forward for oceanic conservation and for helping marine ecosystems adapt to a changing climate, it also poses significant management, budgetary and political challenges.

The challenges start with the site's remoteness, a far remove even from the main Hawaiian Islands, the outer boundary is about sixteen hundred miles from Honolulu, and much further from the West Coast. Obama added more than 440,000 square miles to boost the already designated monument to a staggering 582,578 square miles. Yes, square miles, not acres. This gigantic national monument is larger than all the US national parks and national forests combined. It's almost twice the size of Texas and nearly the area of Alaska.

The conservation mission of Papahānaumokuākea, which is now the largest blue reserve on this blue planet, is also a tall order. Significantly, the mission prohibits fishing and other resource exploitation to protect such endangered species as the short-tailed albatross and the remaining population of Hawaiian monk seals, as well as the long-living black coral, some estimated to be four thousand years old). So little of its flora and fauna have been studied that it's highly likely that the seven thousand species known to inhabit the region are but a fraction of those that inhabit its lands and waters.

The national monument also comes with a social-justice commitment. In an innovative co-management initiative, the state's lead indigenous-rights agency, the Department of Hawaiian Affairs, was tasked with supervising numerous cultural and sacred sites, particularly on the island of Mokumanamana, about four hundred miles northwest of Honolulu. A NOAA report released in late 2020 indicates that this island alone is home to one of the highest densities of sacred sites in the entire Hawaiian Archipelago. By any calculation, Papahānaumokuākea is astonishing.

In comparison, consider that in the early twentieth century the first generation of forest rangers on the US national forests had to patrol a million acres in the remote western mountains. Understandably they were baffled at how they and their horses could steward their new domain. Imagine their modern counterparts trying to survey a waterscape more than three hundred times that extent, even with airplanes and satellites. Papahānaumokuākea dwarfs our faith in management by technology.

The current state of the Pacific Ocean adds another set of problems. Endangered Hawaiian monk seals, green turtles, and seabirds routinely are found in the national monument entangled in derelict fishing gear, including ghost nets and other refuse. The source of these deadly snares is the so-called Great Pacific Garbage Patch, a gyre that captures detritus that has been flushed into the ocean from Pacific Rim industrial-and-consumer economies. *USA Today* reported in Spring 2021 that a multi-agency clean-up crew netted nearly fifty tons of material. "The islands act like a comb that gather debris on its otherwise pristine beaches."

Then there are the sizeable budgetary constraints. All three of the cooperating federal agencies managing Papahānaumokuākea — the National Park Service, US Fish and Wildlife Service, and NOAA — have endured constrained funding for the past several decades. Less-well resourced, they were tasked at the same time with an increased number of properties to oversee; President Obama's rapid-fire creation of thirty-two new or expanded national monuments meant that the Park Service had increased responsibilities without an adequate budget. I understood at the time why the chief executive moved with such dispatch — a mash-up of legacy building and opportunity was knocking. But the speed with which this administration designated these sites, and their disparate fiscal demands, outstripped the executive branch's capacity to underwrite them. Shortly after his inauguration in January 2021, President Biden announced an appropriations package that proposed to resolve issues of deferred maintenance and to accelerate long-delayed restoration projects. Yet Papahānaumokuākea's needs are many and it competes with hundreds of parks, refuges, and sanctuaries.

Preservation politics played a role in the public reaction to the executive order. In the nation's capital, Republican legislators denounced Obama's ready use of the Antiquities Act (1906), even though he was utilizing an executive power that Congress sanctioned more than a century earlier. The partisan nature of their opposition in 2016 surfaced two years later when the GOP gladly acquiesced as President Trump used this same authority to overturn or shrink some of Obama's designations, most notably Bears Ears National Monument in Utah.

From the start, there was also a local test of the federal government's conservation stewardship at Papahānaumokuākea. In the run-up to the Obama designation, the National Park Service held a series of raucous public meetings in which the industrial and longline fishing industry, along with some Indigenous Hawaiian organizations, opposed the designation. Preservation of marine life, they argued, was in direct competition with their long history of harvesting food from these very waters. How the federal agencies manage these fraught human dynamics will be every bit as critical as their stewardship of the marinescape's threatened biodiversity.

At the same time, Papahānaumokuākea's oddly bipartisan political history is buoying. It owes existence to two very different presidents, one whose administration downplayed emerging climate change science, the other who was at the forefront of world leaders responding to the threats that climate change poses.

In 2006, after a White House screening of Jacques-Michel Cousteau's documentary "Voyage to Kure," which details human damage to the islands' ecosystems, President George W. Bush was moved to action. Using the 1906 Antiquities Act, he set aside

Papahānaumokuākea as the first of four parks he would create in the Pacific. *Time* magazine dubbed this collection of sites Bush's last acts of "greenness," while a legion of environmental critics suggested they were his first and last. For the record, at least he did more than his father, George H.W. Bush, one of only three presidents not to designate any national monuments, Reagan and Nixon the other two.

Given how distant the sites that Bush established were from the continental United States, their very isolation may have dampened any national controversy. Still, as *Time* observed, these "marine monuments will mean that President Bush—perhaps the least environmental president in U.S. history—will have protected more of the ocean than anyone else in the world."

Obama blew that claim out of the water. But he did so in a more calculated, less cathartic manner. As part of his 2009 commitment to address climate change, his administration sought projects that would enhance landscape resilience to the effects of climate change. In 2014, for example, he added roughly three hundred thousand square miles to the Bush-inaugurated Pacific Remote Islands Marine National Monument, a stretch of remote Pacific islands south and west of Hawai'i, bringing its total to nearly five hundred thousand square miles. His justification was that its expansion would strengthen Pacific ecosystems. The same rationale was deployed in support of Papahānaumokuākea National Monument.

These two mega-monuments, when combined with the other one hundred twenty six, smaller US marine sanctuaries, now account for about twenty six percent of the nation's waters, meaning that collectively they are giving oceanic species a protected space in which to survive as the climate-charged seas warm and rise. Obama's action in the Pacific was more than a grand gesture. It just might be a planetary life preserver.

Grandmother Ocean

In the foreground: A mature gray whale arcs up and out of the cold Pacific waters, photographed in a classic backward dive. In the background: Lisamu', or Morro Rock, a rust-orange volcanic plug sacred to the Northern Chumash people. It's one of a chain of relict "necks" of extinct volcanoes, lava domes and intrusions visible along the coast of San Luis Obispo County in Central California. The ancient, formidable rock, and the iconic gray whale — a species once almost extirpated, now recovering — have become the apt logo of an important campaign to secure the creation of the Chumash Heritage National Marine Sanctuary. The goal: protect forever the waters of this region.

The driving force behind this ambitious proposal is the Northern Chumash Tribal Council (NCTC). Although the Chumash are not federally recognized, they pressed hard for what they know is a significant designation fully consistent with the their centuries-long stewardship of the riparian corridors, rolling hills, meadows, and slot canyons, not to mention the biodiversity of the slate-gray coastal waters. That they are seeking to appropriate federal law to protect their homelands is a deft expression of David Treuer's argument about who has prior claim on the very concept of land and water stewardship. "As the efforts to assimilate us largely failed and we remained, mostly, in our homelands," the Ojibwe author notes in *The Atlantic,* "Americans have gradually assimilated to *our* cultures, *our* worldview, and *our* modes of connecting to nature. The parks enshrine places, but they also emphasize and prioritize a particular way of interacting with the land." The irony? "America has succeeded in becoming more Indian over the past 245 years rather than the other way around."

That viewpoint may well explain the number of allies who have joined with NCTC to advance its claims. In 2015, with the support of the Sierra Club and the Surfrider Foundation, and with the political muscle of Senators Dianne Feinstein and Kamala Harris and local Representative Salud Carbajal, the NCTC submitted an application for the Chumash Sanctuary to NOAA. Five years later, in October 2020, amid the tense presidential campaign, NOAA extended the nomination for another half-decade. Its decision, declared Fred Collins, chair of the NCTC, was a victory for "thrivability," a central element in his people's cosmology in which "all things connected, all things dreaming together for the abundant life of Grandmother Ocean—for fishermen and fisherwomen, tourists, and all that dwell on the shining, magical, mysterious, majestic coast line of the Chumash Heritage National Marine Sanctuary."

The sanctuary, as proposed, is an encompassing ten thousand square miles. That may seem puny compared to the gargantuan Papahānaumokuākea, but its size and reach have its own integrity. The Chumash sanctuary would stretch from just north of Santa Barbara up the coast to Cambria where it would border the Monterey Bay National Marine Sanctuary and its protective line would thrust thirteen miles into the ocean. Doing so will enable its voluminous size to protect submerged Chumash sacred sites ranging from "villages to solstice alignments 6 to 13 miles offshore." As consequential, the nomination ties these underwater locations with the onshore communities, coastal dunes, wetlands and estuaries, and related sacred sites, many of which date back an estimated ten thousand years. In surfacing this deep history, the nomination ties these past lives to their present-day progeny, an affirmation of the continuing adaptation and resilience of the Chumash people.

All species, then as now, are part of this enduring community. The Santa Lucia Bank, along with a "3,000 meter-deep five-fingered submarine canyon through which the west coast's only persistent upwelling flows," bring up nutrient-rich water to feed marine life, including thirteen species of whales and dolphins. Closer to shore, the vast carbon-absorbing kelp forests harbor otters and seals and fish, while rocky intertidal regions sustain large numbers of pinnipeds and the requisite pupping areas, as well as spawning areas, rookeries and nurseries. The marinescape's extraordinary profusion is a clue as to why the Chumash, then as now, revere these waters of plenty.

They used to be much more plentiful. The decline is linked to the violent dispersal of the Chumash themselves. Spanish missionaries, who penetrated the region in the eighteenth century used colonization and conversion to disrupt the millennia-long relationship between the coastal-savvy people and the ocean world they managed. They were further severed from the places they had lived for untold generations when Americans arrived in the mid-nineteenth century. As happened across what would become the state of California in 1850, whites launched genocidal attacks on remaining Chumash enclaves and appropriated their land. Survivors were roped into the cash economy and became manual laborers on ranches and farms. At the same time, brutal whaling and sealing operations slaughtered thousands of cetaceans and pinnipeds, nearly wiping out these species along the entire west coast. Fish stocks were as devastated. Salmon, steelhead trout, and anchovies, to name a few, were caught, netted, and scooped up, then hauled to large canneries from Morro Bay north to Monterey, from which they distributed around the world.

Shellfish did not escape the ravages of a capitalist-industrializing of the ocean and shore. Abalone, perhaps the most favored of all the Chumash foods, had been routinely harvested by those living on the Channel Islands and the coastal villages. Shells have been found in middens dated back more than twelve thousand years and thus attest to abalone's persistence in their diet; the richly iridescent shells were integral to ceremonies, dances, trade, oral histories and songs, and as decoration for baskets and tomols, the Chumash's plank-built boat. In a post-mission world, however, it became increasingly difficult to access this protein source, and by the late nineteenth century what access there had been became nearly impossible. An abalone "rush" occurred when market demand, investment capital, and the invention of hard-hat dive suits led to a rapid harvest even in deep waters. In 1899, writes Anne Vileisis in her compelling history *Abalone: The Remarkable History and Uncertain Future of California's Iconic Shellfish,* the US Fish Commission estimated that "Japanese fishermen alone harvested 369,411 pounds of dried abalone meat and 525,423 pounds of shells statewide." During the Great Depression of the 1930s, a small clutch of commercial divers based in Morro Bay yanked up more than ten million pounds of abalone.

A century later, abalone's recovery remains uncertain, Vileisis argues, due to "predictions for more marine heat waves, changes in ocean chemistry, and rising risks for disease." Violet Sage-Walker, a member of the Northern Chumash, identified one of these interlocking challenges to then US Representative Deb Haaland, who later was confirmed as Secretary of the Interior in the Biden Administration, the first Indigenous person to hold that important Cabinet post. Sage-Walker wrote in the *San Luis Obispo New Times* in late March 2021 of a wide-ranging conversation with Haaland about the need for tribal land and water sovereignty. "After a traditional exchange where I gave her sage and a baby abalone necklace," Sage-Walker spoke of her people's "efforts to have our ancestral waters protected by designating them a National Marine Sanctuary. I told her my people have witnessed ocean acidification in the Chumash heritage waters, which interferes with abalone's ability to form hard shells as they grow."

Eliminating this local manifestation of acidification, which is mainly the result of carbon dioxide gas in the atmosphere dissolving into the ocean, requires the end of offshore oil-and-gas development. Keeping fossil fuels locked in the earth, as Indigenous Peoples are demanding near other sacred sites like Chaco Canyon National Historic Park in New Mexico, Theodore Roosevelt National Park in North Dakota, and Bears Ears National Monument in Utah, will not alone ensure that abalone once again will proliferate among Pacific Coast reefs and rocks. But it will give them a fighting chance. Just as the formal designation of the sanctuary will further legitimize the Northern Chumash Tribal Council's principled advocacy on behalf of its homelands.

NICHE

Homesteaded

In the lobby of the Claremont Public Library were two temporary displays. One was a small bookstand, holding a clutch of western potboilers from those old dab hands, Zane Grey and Louis L'Amour; a compilation of Max Brand's provocatively titled novels *(Man From Mustang; Six-Gun Country);* and a couple of anthologies of cowboy lit, whose glossy covers and excited prose reinforce the legend of how the West was won — with a smoking Colt 45.

The second display, dubbed "Railroading in Claremont," a contribution of the Santa Fe Railway Historical and Modeling Society, offered up photographs, maps, and ephemera detailing the lengthy relationship between this small college town and the iron rail, dating back to the late nineteenth century.

Although these two modest exhibits seem to have nothing to do with one another, and the library makes nothing of their pairing, in fact they are tightly intertwined as a result of two strokes of Abraham Lincoln's pen in 1862.

Return to the jumble of fiction on that first display's shelf. Its texts may be replete with steel-eyed lawmen, marauding gunslingers, sly rustlers, jilted lovers, and gold-hearted prostitutes but these stock figures had much less to do with the winning of the West than the passage of a piece of congressional legislation whose sesquicentennial this exhibit celebrates — the Homestead Act of 1862 (Public Law 37–64).

On May 20, one hundred and sixty years ago, Abraham Lincoln signed the bill that had been a key campaign pledge during his 1860 run for the White House. He was convinced that opening the public lands would alleviate poverty and stimulate growth. The best way to achieve this, he believed, was to encourage homesteaders to move west, thereby boosting local populations and setting the stage for territories to become states. He shrewdly calculated that the Democratic Party, so weakened when its southern members seceded, could not stop the bill and its support for Republican ideological commitments to Free Soil, Free Labor, Free Men.

The Civil War provided the pretext for a new civil society. Alas, the Homestead Act failed to deliver on its promise. Its intentions were genuine, offering incentives to any citizen (or anyone who intended to become a citizen) to lay claim to upwards of one hundred sixty acres of federally owned land. After making minimal improvements to the property and completing a five-year residence on this cultivated terrain, the occupant, after paying a small registration fee, would own the land free and clear.

As historian Mark Fiege notes in his superb book, *The Republic of Nature,* Lincoln used the nation's "enormous natural strength — its land base — for democratization and development." This generous offer and economic enticement, however, contained a political payback — the Republic-dominated Congress did not extend its provisions to anyone who had "borne arms against the United States Government or given aid and comfort to its enemies." Confederate soldiers and their sympathizers need not apply.

But for those who met the requisite qualifications, and fulfilled the act's provisions, homesteading could be a boon. One of the first claimants was the aptly named Daniel Freeman, a Civil War veteran, who secured lands near Beatrice, Nebraska, where he and his family farmed and ranched. His former acreage is now the location of the Homestead National Monument, dedicated to the people whose lives the Homestead Act fundamentally altered.

There is, however, much more to this legislation than the boost it gave to stalwart settler-colonists. Because the Homestead Act's language was so cumbersome, and so thoroughly riddled with legal loopholes, its stated intent—to populate the west with yeoman farm families, the original American Dream from Jefferson to Lincoln—proved of secondary importance.

Instead, wringing the greatest benefits from Honest Abe's law were big corporations and major speculators, not the common man and woman it was intended to serve and secure. True, appropriate safeguards had been set (Warning: take a deep breath before reading this run-on sentence):

> That the person applying for the benefit of this act shall, upon application to the register of the land office in which he or she is about to make such entry, make affidavit before the said register or receiver that he or she is the head of a family, or is twenty-one years or more of age, or shall have performed service in the army or navy of the United States, and that he has never borne arms against the Government of the United States or given aid and comfort to its enemies, and that such application is made for his or her exclusive use and benefit, and that said entry is made for the purpose of

> actual settlement and cultivation, and not either directly
> or indirectly for the use or benefit of any other person or
> persons whomsoever; and upon filing the said affidavit
> with the register or receiver, and on payment of ten
> dollars, he or she shall thereupon be permitted to enter
> the quantity of land specified ...

Got that? Good. Now things get complicated, as the legal caveats pile up: Each party depended on the vigilance, honesty, and goodwill of any number of agents involved in these transactions (breathe deep once more):

> ... no [land ownership] certificate shall be given or patent
> issued therefore until the expiration of five years from the
> date of such entry; and if, at the expiration of such time,
> or at any time within two years thereafter, the person
> making such entry; or, if he be dead, his widow; or in
> case of her death, his heirs or devisee; or in case of a
> widow making such entry, her heirs or devisee, in case of
> her death; shall prove by two credible witnesses that he,
> she, or they have resided upon or cultivated the same for
> the term of five years immediately succeeding the time of
> filing the affidavit aforesaid, and shall make affidavit that
> no part of said land has been alienated, and that he has
> borne true allegiance to the Government of the United
> States; then, in such case, he, she, or they, if at that time
> a citizen of the United States, shall be entitled to a patent,
> as in other cases provided for by law ...

For the guileful—and there were many of them in the war's chaotic aftermath—this convoluted prose provided ample opportunities to swindle the nation out of some of its most resource-rich lands. Logging companies, ranching operations, mining concerns, and railroad conglomerates bribed federal agents to get what they wanted, or paid people to claim lands that they then handed over to the syndicates.

These scams were astonishingly effective. Of the five hundred million acres of public land that Department of the Interior's General Land Office gave away between 1862 and 1904, only about eighty million went to those for whom it was intended. Well-capitalized organizations and nefarious speculators snatched up the other 420 million, which they stripped for its timber, grass, or minerals before moving on to their next spoil.

Gifford Pinchot, the first chief of the Forest Service, founded in 1905 to manage many of these abandoned landscapes, lamented that "the vast common heritage of land fit for and intended for American homes," had fallen into the "crooked, mercenary, and speculative hands of companies, corporations, and monopolies."

The consequences were staggering, he concluded. America's natural resources, "with whose conservation and use the whole future of the Nation was bound up, were passing under the control of men who developed and destroyed them with one and only one object in mind—their own personal profit." Within forty years of its passage, the Homestead Act's democratic impulse had been perverted.

This is not to say that the legislation offered no economic benefits to individuals. Rather, it's that a minority took the lion's share of this newfound wealth, further skewing the inequities that already plagued the United States. The rich got very much richer.

Leading this selfish pursuit was the prime beneficiary of free public lands, the transcontinental railroads. Two months after he signed the Homestead Act, Lincoln put his signature to the Pacific

Railway Act (1862) (12 Stat. 489), the purpose of which was to tie California to the Union.

This was the first of many such massive giveaways. While it's true that building rail systems to carry people and goods across the country required massive federal support, it's also fair to note that most of the millions of acres these companies received were not essential to constructing these transcontinental corridors. Rather, the acres were critical to the creation of whistle-stop towns along the routes that would become home to commercial nodes and residences radiating out from the tracks.

Public lands were given to private interests who sold the property back to the public, a neat and very profitable trick. Those tidy profits were redoubled when these residents, now utterly dependent on this sole source of transit to eastern markets, had to pay inflated prices as passengers, producers, and consumers. This is what it means to be "railroaded."

One such kept town was Claremont, California. In the late 1880s, as the Santa Fe railroad laid down tracks between San Bernardino and Los Angeles, it emerged as one of thirty or so new town sites. Consistent with the pattern with such land schemes nationally, promoters drew up a beguiling panoramic map that laid out what the prospective community would look like, straight lines expanding out from the depot and into a prosperous future. A prime example of blue-sky cartography.

For a time, land sales were brisk, as illustrated in the photo of the local Santa Fe station surrounded by horse-drawn wagons whose owners were gathered for an auction. The PR was just as inflated. Promised one pitch: Claremont was "The Leading Townsite on the Santa Fe Route."

Soon enough the bubble collapsed, and land prices might have remained deflated but for a clever real-estate agent who offered the Claremont Hotel and a good number of unsold lots to lure a recently established college away from the nearby city of Pomona. When in 1889 Pomona College moved to its present site, the railroad had its first important customer. This small economic base expanded quickly with the planting of citrus groves throughout Southern California, whose fragrance enveloped Claremont and whose fruits fueled its commercial activity for the next sixty years.

Without the Homestead and Pacific Railroad acts, this one community and countless others like it across the region would not exist. These legislative initiatives, and not a six-shooter or tin badge, was how the modern West was made.

Defensible Space

My first brush with the life-threatening nature of western wildfires came on a sizzling-hot day in October 1973, shortly after starting my junior year at Pitzer College in Claremont, California. A good friend, John Warfel, then living in a dilapidated cabin in Palmer Canyon in the city's rumpled northern foothills, had been asked by his landlord to clear space around the structure in case fire swept across the landscape. Channeling Tom Sawyer, John regaled a group of Eastern transplants with the joys of cutting back chamise, sage, yucca, and other shrubs, trimming scrub oaks, and hacking through sharp-bladed grasses. He forgot to mention poison oak. By the end of the day, we were dehydrated, sunburned, and red-rashed, but had succeeded in opening up about a one-hundred-foot swath.

The poison-oak scars remain, as does the chilling realization that that ramshackle abode, if still standing thirty years later, would have burned in October 2003 when the Padua Fire tore through Palmer Canyon. That fire, part of the Old/Grand Prix complex, burned through more than ninety thousand acres, enough land for twenty-five hundred Pitzers, on the southern slopes of the San Bernardino and San Gabriel Mountains in Southern California. It killed six people, torched nearly a thousand homes, and forced eighty thousand to evacuate. Palmer Canyon may have been a small part of this inferno, one of fifteen wildfires burning across the region that fall, but nearly every single structure in that remote, oak-embowered site was destroyed.

Since then, Claremont's hillsides have been relatively wildfire-free. The city's good fortune could change in a moment, as the December 2017 quartet of fires—the Thomas, Creek, Rye, and Skirball—reminds. The climate-charged lengthening of Southern California's fire season and the drought-desiccated landscape fuels these fires and someday again will turn our skies black. In anticipation of that dark day, now would be a good time to decrease, where possible, the odds of another devastating Padua fire.

In light of these odds, the Clara Oaks development—forty-plus luxury homes proposed to be built above Claremont's Webb Canyon on a site that Cal Fire has designated a High Severity Fire Zone—will prove disastrous. If the Planning Commission and the City Council greenlight the project, they'll be responsible for placing its future residents directly and inevitably in harm's way. They'll also be sanctioning the devastation of a hundred-acre swath of irreplaceable wildland habitat.

This is not an over-the-top claim but is based on my more than two decades of research, writing, and teaching about wildland fire in the western United States. That work leads me to the simple and grim conclusion that the Clara Oaks project, accessed by a narrow road and situated in our flammable foothills, will burn. When it does, it will rival the destructive fury of the 2003 Padua/Grand Prix fire that incinerated Palmer Canyon and portions of the residential area Claraboya.

Because our foothills and mountains have not had a major fire in nearly twenty years, inland Southern California and Claremont are flashpoints. The return-fire cycle for chaparral is roughly fifteen to twenty-five years, and because chaparral dominates the Clara Oaks site and its surroundings, odds are that this landscape will burn sooner rather than later.

Constructing Clara Oaks will heighten this risk. A recent Forest Service scientific paper notes that houses built in the wildland-urban interface (WUI) act as accelerants. One of its key findings is that "settled areas with little wildland vegetation that are near large blocks of wildland vegetation [are] where the greatest total amount of building destruction has occurred in California." The Clara Oaks site matches that description — it abuts the Claremont Hills Wilderness Park and County and Federal wildlands. Fire in one area will mean fire in another.

This is especially true when combustible structures are in place. Houses, cars, propane tanks and high-voltage wires have routinely touched off wildfires or energized them. The 2020 Bobcat Fire, previously described, resulted from a SoCal Edison overhead conductor. Two major utilities' wires run just north of Clara Oaks. Sparks cascading from a Golden State Water Company's chop-saw ignited the 2013 Foothill Fire that burned the Bernard Field Station. Construction accidents are a constant threat in this area.

Clara Oaks would add to this disturbing legacy. Section 3.17-Transportation of the Initial Study reveals the project's failure to conform with California Environmental Quality Act climate-mitigation requirements. These issues are central to the state's precedent-setting intervention in a lawsuit against Lake County's flawed Environmental Impact Report for a major development in a High Severity Fire Zone. Clara Oaks would be a prime target for similar litigation.

Of greater concern are the unacknowledged dangers residents and firefighters will face on Webb Canyon Road when a fire erupts in the hillsides. The steep-walled topography will channel the wind-driven flames southward and its furious run will collide with the human geography—the single, narrow road with a pinch-point bridge that leads to safety. Even if Clara Oaks evacuees manage to escape via the development's curving, smoke-filled streets, they will be caught behind their fleeing downhill neighbors. The resulting gridlock will block fire engines dispatched to fight the inferno. We don't need more post-wildfire photographs of burned-out vehicles littering roads once perceived as escape routes.

Clara Oaks, in short, fails to meet city, county, and state requirements. The Claremont Planning Commission and City Council need no other grounds to reject the proposed development outright. Doing so will protect the community's safety, health and welfare while preserving its natural heritage.

Air Flow

Watching a community wake up, and its routinized choreography, is part of what has made my daily walk up Mountain Avenue, which bisects my Claremont Village-adjacent neighborhood, so engrossing. Groggy commuters back down their driveways, their cars' headlights flicker past as they speed toward Foothill Boulevard, on their way to the 210 Freeway. Dodging the ubiquitous irrigation spray (only some of which lands on the intended lawns and landscaping), bicyclists, joggers, and dog-walkers move through the shadows. Sleepy-headed neighbors wheel trashcans to the curbside while parents drop off their pre-school kids at Claremont Presbyterian and North Hills Adventist churches or older children at Mountain View and Condit Elementary Schools. The day has begun.

As beguiling as its commencement appears, there's a dark lining to this pretty picture of suburban domesticity. The air we are breathing outdoors, in our homes, and at school is not as clear as it may appear. That's what researchers from UCLA and the California Air Resources Board, who monitored auto-emission levels at the overpass at Mountain and 210 and then tracked its flow downhill, have argued. Their results have forced me to rethink when I get up and where I walk.

Until this study's results were released in *Atmospheric Environment,* urban planners, public officials, and real-estate agents assumed that if you lived within a thousand feet of a freeway you would inhale considerably more toxic air than if you lived farther away. Now we learn that worrisome pollution plume extends upwards of a mile or more from its freeway-generated source — in short, five times farther than previously had been believed.

To establish this point, researchers drove a zero-emission vehicle mounted with an array of sensitive instruments to measure ultrafine particles and calculate the presence of those bad boys of air pollution — carbon monoxide and nitric oxide — along surface streets that run perpendicular to a series of heavily trafficked freeways in the Los Angeles region. Rather than taking measurements during peak rush hours, morning and afternoon, they selected 4:30 to 6:30 a.m. as their timeframe.

They discovered these early hours prove critical to the spread of this plume of bad air into the built environment. This stretch is a consequence of the typical overnight cooling in Southern California that leads to what is called a nocturnal surface inversion. It traps vehicular-generated pollution close to the ground and then breezes move the concentrated soup downwind. This nocturnal boundary layer does not decay until after the sun rises, the atmosphere heats, and the winds kick up, mixing this unhealthy low-lying plume with cleaner air above.

"This is happening around every freeway," says project head Suzanne Paulson of UCLA's Department of Atmospheric and Oceanic Sciences, "and a similar situation likely happens around the world in the early morning hours. The particles tend to end up indoors, so a lot of people are being exposed inside their homes and schools."

Given that an estimated twenty-five percent of the Southland's population lives within this danger zone, millions of its residents in single-family homes, multiplexes, and apartments, are directly affected. Including a lot of those who reside in Claremont.

Our home, for example, sits within the zone of greatest impact — one mile south of the traffic-jammed 210 Freeway. As the UCLA research reveals, what makes southerly residences, schools, and business in 91711 more vulnerable than those to the north of the freeway are the prevailing breezes. "The early morning air flow at the overpass of Mountain Avenue and the 210 is "the least variable [in the study] due to the adjacent [San Gabriel] mountains to the north which produce a strong, thermally-induced, mountain-valley wind system."

The very weather pattern that's made my early morning walks seem so refreshing, so salubrious, has been compromising my health and that of a lot of others. I've had to adapt. Instead of pushing north at dawn's early light, more frequently I turn south, and then fan out west or east, a new route and routine that's a good deal better than the alternative of not exercising — or not breathing.

Concrete Loss

It happened when I wasn't even looking. When some noisy combination of jackhammer, backhoe, and compact dozer tore apart a section of curb-and-sidewalk along Foothill Boulevard close to Wolfe's Market, grinding into rubble a marker of Claremont's history.

That's not a criticism, because unless you were really searching for it you would have missed this near-invisible imprint, a small date-stamp that signaled when this stretch of street infrastructure originally had been constructed. Fortunately, when I spotted the stamp in late 2018, after years of walking along that same route and never seeing what suddenly seemed glaringly obvious, I took a photograph. The text was easier to decipher in real-time than in the grainy image, but it reads:

Griffith Company
1928

The company, which today bills itself as one of California's "earliest general contractors" was founded in 1902 and incorporated six years before its workers built the sidewalk on the south side of the busy thoroughfare. Fascinatingly, over one hundred years later the company bid on the Foothill Boulevard Improvement Project. The original laborers did a good job, as the concrete they poured stood up to ninety years of use and abuse. Until, that is, it was broken up, trucked away, and, hopefully, ground down to be recycled into some other streetscape. Dust to dust.

This particulate matter may be a clue to the source of materials that Griffith Company mixed to build that no-longer extant sidewalk. "Prior to the development of inexpensive modern asphalt in the 1920s, cities struggled to find affordable, durable, and available types of pavement suitable to their needs," observed Robin B. Williams, an architectural historian at Savannah College of Art and Design. As a result, "pavement was inherently local," a site-specific character that led Williams to launch Historic Pavement, a compelling website devoted to documenting "examples of diverse street and sidewalk pavement types, embedded features (such as street signs and commercial advertisements), and curbs, as well as developing city profiles."

Claremont would make an intriguing case study for Historic Pavement, given our region's alluvial soils and the major quarrying operations that continue to mine nearby San Antonio Wash. Just as it does today, in 1928 it would have made sense (and cents) for the Griffith Company to excavate this nearby resource for its infrastructure project. That one of its employees then pressed the company's name and time stamp into the not-yet-set concrete, and that this emblem survived for as long as it did, says something about its elemental durability.

Other such signifiers endure across Claremont. Without intending to, one morning while strolling mid-street I looked down and to the right. In the gutter I spotted another "Griffith Company 1928" stamp close to my first sighting. Over the next two weeks, I

The next two decades brought mid-century ranch homes west of Mountain Avenue, north of Foothill, and south of Arrow Highway, a pattern of outward expansion that subsequently flattened the remaining orange groves as development pressed ever farther north. It's simple enough to trace these new subdivisions and anchoring institutions. In 1965, Martin & Jewett had a lock on building the sidewalk-curb-and-gutter infrastructure along the west side of Mountain. Its crews imprinted the company name and year in curb cuts to El Roble Intermediate School (opened in 1964), Claremont Presbyterian Church (1960), and Mountain View Elementary (1962).

Three years later this same firm secured the contract for one of the city's most controversial road-building projects—the four-lane Claremont Boulevard that bisected the longstanding Arbor Verde neighborhood. This compact community was home to hundreds of Latino families, many of whom had initially found employment in local groves and orchards or joined the workforce of the Claremont Colleges. This community, writes historian Matt Garcia in *A World of Its Own* (2002), was marginalized physically, straddling the Los Angeles-San Bernardino County line, and unincorporated in each. The residents were ignored in terms of health and public services, as were those living in barrios and colonias across the US Southwest. For instance, Arbor Verde received no water or sewer hookups or other essential utilities. The residents were also marginalized socially, hemmed in by Claremont's restrictive residential covenants. Garcia quoted Mexican American journalist and civil rights leader Ignacio López who described Arbor Verde as "tierra de nadie"—land of no one. Ramming Claremont Boulevard through the community, dismantling the neighborhood's Catholic Church, uprooting countless families and severing their kin and social networks, all the while locking a new streetscape into place with Martin & Jewett-poured sidewalks and curbs, was just one more compiling indignity.

On the city's expanding northern rim, on what developers liked to call "raw" land, the construction of new subdivisions tied together by streets and sidewalks did not roll out with uniformity. Like the game of hopscotch, the construction of homes and walkways leaped from one site and acre to another. The availability of land and capital determined where, when, and how developers built. Date-stamps along a quarter mile stretch of Scripps Avenue, an east-west arterial north of Foothill, indicate that two different companies built the northside sidewalks over a four-year period. The first two of blocks were set in place in 1961, the western half of the third in 1963, the eastern half in 1965. The fourth also dated from 1965. Then there are the juxtaposing dates and contractors of two abutting sidewalk stamps on East College Way in the Piedmont Mesa neighborhood—one from 1959, the other 1961.

This gap in construction may have been only a minor inconvenience to the subdivision's early residents, but it offers a significant insight into the mechanism by which the built landscape was snapped together like Legos, one sidewalk, curb, and gutter at a time. Look down: a vital part of the community's complicated historical record has been hiding in plain sight.

Code Green

What do buildings mean? How do their volume, mass, and detail convey their subject and significance? How do their materials evoke and provoke, or signal what we should see and think about their form and function? And should residences or commercial structures or civic centers or skyscrapers stand for something?

The US Green Building Council (USGBC) believes so. Since its founding in 1993, the non-profit organization has been a relentless promoter of the idea that a building's design should be a sustainable as possible, and that sustainability is a key index of its value and meaning. USGBC's incentive-based metric assessing a design is its rating system known as LEED (Leadership in Energy and Environmental Design). For architects, developers, and contractors—and their clients—LEED has become a Good Housekeeping Seal of Approval.

And a way of keeping score—the more points a structure earns towards its LEED certification, the more lustrous the medal bestowed. While there's nothing wrong with securing Silver or Gold, Platinum is the ultimate benchmark, a shining example of how the construction industry might help make the world a more habitable place.

Or not. LEED's many critics are wary of the system's low bar for certification, arguing that it asks too little of its applicants, offering instead a grade-inflated set of outcomes that undercuts their value. Critics are also skeptical about LEED's failure to require post-construction assessment of how certified buildings function: are they as good as advertised? As efficient? As low impact? An even greater lack in the rating is an analysis of how people interact with these certified buildings in real-time. All that glitters is not gold. Or platinum.

Yet in this vein the debate is healthy, especially if it compels producers and consumers to ask sharper questions about the built landscape we inhabit, about why it looks, feels, and operates as it does. I contributed a small bit to this larger discussion when I spoke at the dedication of Pomona College's two new dormitories in 2011, shortly after they achieved the highest level of LEED certification. They earned it too; they're not fool's gold.

For those of us of a certain age Sontag and Dialynas residential halls are more than a little mind-boggling. Let me put it this way. If you graduated in the last century, or if, as was then often the case, cinder-block construction was the height of your dorm's fashion, then these well-appointed buildings are almost incomprehensible. If a thin coat of institutional-bland paint was slapped on your dorm, inside and out, then you'll be baffled to know that what was once a utilitarian structure now comes complete with a color scheme.

Color us green with envy.

That's the right hue in another sense. These two buildings could not be greener, more technically sweet, or more sustainable. Rooted in the physical landscape, they will also make an essential contribution to the human ecology of this particular academic community—something that LEED does not yet measure.

Naturally, the college takes a lot of pride in these upscale buildings and has posted online an extensive list of their more remarkable attributes. I want to point out one that, I confess, speaks to my inner wonk—stormwater control. Hardly as sexy as the array of solar panels, lacking the cachet of the green roof and garden, and not nearly as cool as the energy efficiencies that are built into the halls' every design element, the stormwater system is arguably more revolutionary.

To understand why, imagine a single raindrop hurtling down during one of Southern California's furious late-winter storms. The moment it hits the ground, according to those who have engineered the Los Angeles basin since the late nineteenth-century, it should be captured as quickly as possible behind a dam or in a ditch or culvert, then swiftly channeled into the concrete-lined Santa Ana, San Gabriel, or Los Angeles rivers before being flushed ignominiously into the sea.

This complex system, designed to prevent flooding, has wreaked havoc with riparian ecosystems, destroying the once-robust regional runs of steelhead trout. It also has severely limited the capacity of nature to replenish local groundwater supplies. We have compensated for this loss—thanks to William Mulholland and his ilk—by expropriating snowmelt from as far away as the northern Rockies.

Sontag and Dialynas dormitories embody a much smarter, locally framed, approach. Any precipitation that falls within, or flows through, their catchment area will be retained onsite, and filtered down to a large underground detention basin in the alluvial wash that runs along the campus' eastern edge. There it will slowly percolate into the aquifer, recharging the Pomona Valley's groundwater. In so doing, these two dormitories benefit and befit their environment.

Yet will they be as integrative as human habitats? How will generations of students occupy these dorms and make them their own? How will they respond to these buildings that teach sustainability every time they flick a light switch, open a window, or flush a toilet, but that also require their active participation to insure its realization?

These are some of the questions my students and I wrestled with in the preceding week as we read Alain de Botton's compelling text, *The Architecture of Happiness* (2006). Among his suggestive insights is this gem: "Belief in the significance of architecture is premised on the notion that we are, for better or worse, different people in different places—and on the conviction that it is architecture's task to render vivid to us who we might ideally be."

We won't know whether Sontag and Dialynas halls will serve this beneficent function until we conduct longitudinal studies of how these buildings are used, how they are reimagined through the students' daily interactions with them. Although one wag offered this early critique in an essay in which he employed de Botton's typologies to critique the buildings, dubbing them "upper-class housing where lonely seniors go to graduate."

Examining this range of reactions—from hopeful to hyperbolic—was a pair of seniors in the Environmental Analysis program who wrote their theses on the new dorms' social dynamics and structural innovations, and the interplay between them. Their work, when combined with three other research projects assessing different aspects of the relationship between Pomona's built landscape and its lived reality, were the first attempts to deepen our understanding of how this Claremont campus actually functions for those who call it home.

There is another reason why the logistics and operations of these edifices must be questioned. Pomona College has asserted that sustainability is integral to its modern mission. One mark of its commitment has been the establishment of a Sustainability Integration Office — the middle word is of prime importance — that inculcates sustainable concepts into new construction and the rehabilitation of older facilities and infuses them into the college's curricular goals and extra-curricular activities.

The community must measure the steps it has taken — or should take — to fulfill its convictions. That includes using the intellectual tools and analytical methodologies its professors and students engage with in their classrooms to evaluate the very buildings in which so many abide and work.

But this will only succeed if the investigators are mindful of what de Botton cautions are architecture's limitations and which apply with equal force to the concept of sustainability. "Even at its most accomplished architecture will only ever constitute a small, and imperfect (expensive, prone to destruction and morally unreliable), protest against the state of things."

However limited, this rigorous self-examination is not just an academic exercise. Whatever the results, the evaluations will help us calibrate the human capacity to sustain ourselves on this planet of swelling population and finite resources.

Such calibrations may be especially impactful at the local level. How apt, then, that my students' probing analyses of sustainability as fact and fancy — like the munificence of the donor families that made these two dormitories possible — is fully consistent with, indeed is ineluctably linked to, Pomona College's century-old charge to its graduates: "They only are loyal to this college who, departing, bear their added riches in trust for mankind."

With the Sontag and Dialynas residential halls, the college has reframed that sense of individual social obligation, acknowledging that as an institution it too has a responsibility to redeem this historic pledge.

Build Up

In the early morning hours, as dawn begins to break, Claremont comes alive.

Nowhere is this more obvious than along First Street. Folks living in the townhomes head east, duck into the Packing House for a cup of coffee, and then stroll to the depot to ride a bus or hop Metrolink trains to their jobs. Others, walking south along Indian Hill, Yale, and Harvard slip into their favorite cafe before catching public transit. There, they are joined by folks walking up from South Claremont, and others parking in the Metrolink lot for their daily commute. As they board, others descend and head to the stores, restaurants, and colleges where they are employed.

This energetic and energizing bustle is one of the reasons why many of the community's caffeine-starved daily congregate at the outdoor tables and benches that line the village proper. Their steady patronage keeps bakers and baristas busy.

In this busy-ness lies the message that Claremont has a robust set of Transit-Oriented Developments (TODs). The building blocks are clearly visible. Courier Place and Claremont Villas Senior Apartments abut the railroad tracks on the south. The West Village development lines the north side of the tracks. Each is easily accessible to mass transit. Each adds much-needed density to the city's housing portfolio. The West Village embodies key principles of New Urbanist design by combining living, working, and shopping within a pedestrian landscape.

Village South will function in the exact same way. The proposed TOD will rehab the former industrial and commercial area slotted between Indian Hill Boulevard on the east, the rail tracks to the north, and Bucknell Street on the west. It will activate an area of relatively abandoned acres, precisely as Village West did for the one-time citrus trans-shipment center. As the development builds up and increases density—essential features of TODs—Village South's crucial mix of market-priced and affordable units will integrate living spaces with gardens and plazas. Its proposed boutiques, cafes, and restaurants will bolster the city's tax base. These and other quality-of-life amenities will link residents to bus, train, and soon enough the Metro Gold Line connecting Claremont with Los Angeles through Pasadena. Local cash registers will be ringing and downtown will be jumping.

While Village South will strengthen the contemporary streetscape, it also dovetails with Claremont's urban history as a transit-oriented development. In 1887, the Pacific Land Improvement Company, a subsidiary of the Santa Fe Railroad, platted "the Leading Townsite on the Great Santa Fe Route." Through its First Street sales office, located opposite the original depot, its agents sold lots structured within a classic street gridiron. That pattern created a compact community that radiated out from but remained close to the railroad.

Although it would take time for the blue-sky visions of the town to be realized, business picked up when Pomona College set up shop in the Hotel Claremont in 1889 and fourteen years later its vibrant outlines were established. So much so that in 1903 President Theodore Roosevelt stepped off his whistle-stop tour of the western states, took a short carriage ride to the college's Pearsons Hall, and delivered a stemwinding speech to an estimated seven thousand people.

"My friends and fellow-citizens," the twenty-sixth president thundered, "it is such a pleasure to be in this college town today. It is so wonderful a thing to look at the country through which I have come, to realize that the site of this college but a few years ago was exactly as the rest of the plain was, to realize that all of the cultivation that I see, all of the agricultural work that has been done, that has so completely changed the face of the country, has been done within this brief space of time." Through its spatial and economic development, Claremont was contributing to the state's "foundation of material prosperity."

Because Village South will be woven into the city's historic fabric, the latest expression of its developmental DNA, it will contribute immeasurably to Claremont's twenty-first century urban dynamism. Perhaps best witnessed in the early morning hours, when dawn begins to break.

Re-righting the City

Second Home, an innovative co-working space in Hollywood, has garnered a lot of attention due to its design features. Sixty pods, which occupy a large, former parking lot, are embowered with trees, their interior and exteriors are fancifully painted, and each contains large workable windows that produce a sun-drenched environment for those settling in for a long day's work. As its designer assured the *Los Angeles Times,* "One of the best aspects of living in L.A. is to be able to open a door and being surrounded by nature." The region's "close relationship with the good weather, hummingbirds and flowers is lost if you have stairs, elevators or corridors in the way. The goal was to work in a garden, where you can be indoors, but the outdoors is just a door away."

But is Second Home, as has been touted, a sign of our post-pandemic future? The question also might be asked of the al fresco dining craze, in which restaurants and bakeries have crowded out onto sidewalks in many cities including Claremont. Or commandeered downtown parking spaces and turned them into patios. Or slotted bollards into streets to divert traffic and produce instant pedestrian malls in central cities and small downtowns as has Claremont.

It's not yet clear whether quick adaptations and easy interpolations will do more than provide a rapid influx of consumers and cash to prop up faltering economies and boost employment amid a Covid-sluggish economy. These two results are essential, and in the case of my town, successful, to judge by how few stores and restaurants lost their leases during the pandemic. But I'm not convinced the design interventions by themselves offer long-term solutions to the many and enduring social issues that plagued American cities before the pandemic and which Covid 19's fatal power has further exposed.

By early October 2020, the novel coronavirus had killed more than two hundred thousand Americans, roughly twenty percent of fatalities worldwide. Then by October 2021, tragically more than three times that number had died. Those shocking deaths have a decidedly urban framing. Los Angeles, like New York City, Boston, and Chicago, has been among the epicenters in the United States, a location-concentration that seems consistent across the globe.

Within urban America, some residents have been more impacted than others. The data are glaringly obvious in showing who has died, where, and why. In large part the deaths are correlated with age, race and ethnicity, poverty, class, education, and zip code. The pandemic, in short, has exposed the fault lines that run through US society. These fissures — which include spatial inequities, economic disparities, and political inequalities — have segmented the urban landscape.

In this unsettling context, social distancing takes on new meaning. The same can be said of Second Home's chic if segregated pods, which only reinforce the fragmented, exclusive character of the modern workplace.

How might we intervene more forcefully to correct the inequalities hammered into our built environments? That was one of a series of questions my students and I grappled during the Covid years: Who has rights to the city? Who has unfettered access to a community's public resources—its politics, policies, and services, its streets and open space, its healthy and full life?

Social theorist Henri Lefebvre was an earlier source of some these queries which he used to directly confront the capitalist state that was busily commodifying social relations and controlling city governments. The only effective antidote, Lefebvre argued in *The Right to the City* (1968), was a concerted effort to rescue "the citizen as main element and protagonist of the city that he himself had built" and the subsequent reclamation of the metropolis as "a meeting point for building collective life."

His formative concerns have gained greater urgency amid the global pandemic, but whether they will gain traction is another matter. The news is not particularly encouraging, a point some of my students made when I queried them during the summer of 2020 about what they were observing, thinking, and reading. Luba Masliy sent me a link to architectural critic Benjamin Bratton's sharp interrogation of the pandemic's hollowing out of communal life: "As amenities that were once known as places in the city are transformed now into apps and appliances inside the home, public space is evacuated and the 'domestic' sphere becomes its own horizon."

This relentlessly inward focus has occurred even in highly centralized Moscow, Masliy noted of her hometown. Although its downtown contains the majority of the region's urban functions—jobs, education, shopping, and recreation—it was diminished in one key sense. Before the pandemic, mass-transit rush hours dominated daily commutes. Now, auto-owning Moscovites avoiding mass transit clog the road. She was skeptical whether this gridlock will fuel demand for a more decentralized urban system and greater diversity of infrastructure and services.

Pauline Bekkers shared Masliy's skepticism. She spent the summer back in the Netherlands and there observed a sharp uptick in the number of motorized vehicles on highways, despite her country's longstanding investment in a robust bicycle-and-transit system. "People have such a negative image of public transportation," she wrote, that "they'd rather take any other alternative." Her hope was tempered though, saying, "As much as this is an opportunity for city governments to make radical changes in the urban landscape, it is also essential that we grab this opportunity to change attitudes." Starting with a real commitment to engage with the most vulnerable communities, a goal that required urban planners "to completely reimagine what their planning process looks like and how they empower communities to build their own post-pandemic cities."

That same argument is central to Samuel Stein's *Capital City: Gentrification and the Real Estate State* (2019) which Anam Mehta encouraged me to read. For Stein, the rise of the "real estate state," a phenomenon he associates with New York and other global cities, is attributable to a rapid accumulation of real-estate capital since the 1980s. This concentration of wealth, he writes in homage to Lefebvre's earlier insights, has secured "inordinate influence over the shape of our cities, the parameters of our politics and the lives we lead."

To break that pattern, planners and designers must envision a new and healthier urban society. That potential comes with a catch. The real estate state "is most firmly grafted onto municipal governments,"

Stein observes, "because that is where much of the capitalist state's physical planning is done." This locus means that planners are "uniquely positioned at the nexus of the state, capital and popular power" and as a result they "sit uncomfortably at the center of this maelstrom." The only force that can help these professionals "unwind real estate's grip over our politics," and give them the freedom to dismantle the social inequities built into the urban fabric, is the formation of a series of "mass movements to remake our cities from the ground up."

Were that to occur, then this galvanizing momentum might finally secure Lefebvre's imagined community and our collective and embodied right, in Claremont and elsewhere, to communities that are habitable and just. An outcome that is as essential whether we are locked down or opened up.

Growing Native

Ralph Cornell (1890–1972) spent a lifetime figuring out how things grow. How plants, indigenous and exotic, respond to Southern California's soils, light, and moisture, to its heat and drought. How best to design plazas, parks, and campuses, neighborhoods, and gardens such that their vegetation would nourish those strolling through these restful landscapes. Delights to the eye and soul, Cornell built many civic, collegiate, and communal projects across the Southland.

Consulting arborist Cy Carlberg taught me how to read these key elements in one particular Cornell-inflected space. We were standing on the west end of Marston Quad, Pomona College's iconic greensward and she had me focus not on the sweep of lawn, not on the large buildings anchoring its cardinal points, but on the scattered clustering of sycamores *(Platanus occidentalis)*. Their soaring height lifts our eyes, she observed, and gives volume to what could seem but flat ground. Their mottled, flaking bark counters the monochromatic grass. But more importantly, the copse provides shady dens, cubbies where students can sprawl on the lawn or prop themselves up against the trunks — to sleep, perhaps to dream.

The Quad owes much of its impetus to the framing device that Thomas Jefferson deployed at the University of Virginia. But its arboreal coziness and domestic feel, as writer (and Pomona alum) Verlyn Klinkenborg calls its "laconic beauty," draws from Cornell's undergraduate experience at Pomona, and from which he graduated in 1914. He made his alma mater homier.

Two years before Cornell graduated, he published an article in the *Journal of Economic Botany* proposing a radical re-thinking of landscape design in Southern California. It was so radical that it remains on the cutting edge more than a century later.

The concept he advocated in "Wanted: A Genuine Southern California Park" was simple in its re-orientation. Cornell urged designers and their clients in the region to stop importing plants from wetter climes that were not suited or adaptable to Southern California's arid, sun-drenched environment that was often wracked by drought. Instead, he championed the planting of "native trees, plants, and flowers." What grew along inland foothills, valley floors, and coastal plains would be ideal for residential backyards as well as in city and county parks.

"What could be more interesting and educational," he allowed, "than a public park devoted to plants indigenous to our dry and semi-arid lands, and representative of the many forms of plant life that are found along our coast slopes? A dry ground park, planted only to native trees, shrubs and flowers, would be one of the greatest possible assets to Southern California." Adopting such materials as ceanothus, juniper, and yucca, Spanish bayonet, madrono, and fuschias, oaks, and sycamores, and the native color palette they embodied, would also distinguish the Southland from other parts of the country. Why recreate the East when the West had so much to offer?

Embedded in his query was the profound realization that to live sustainably in Southern California's hot, desiccated environment required adapting to its rigorous climate. "A city very often purchases dry hillsides or rugged slopes for park purposes," he noted. Once having done so, the community feels compelled to install an "elaborate water system ... at enormous expense, and plants entirely foreign to such an environment are grotesquely perched where they must serve a life-long sentence of struggle for existence under conditions entirely adverse to their best development." In short, native plants would survive better and there was little need for irrigation and thus no pressure for imported water.

The issue of importing water was of intense concern and daily conversation in the region at the time. Even as Cornell wrote his manifesto, Los Angeles was building its controversial aqueduct from Owens Valley, a structure that ushered in an era of cheap water and the offered possibility of a lush, hyper-green landscape in this sere-brown terrain.

Cornell challenged some of the aesthetic presumptions and political calculations of his time, and his insights also identified the choices that planners, designers, and citizens now face in the early twenty-first century. In an age of climate disruption, intense drought, and escalating cost of water funneled into the region from the northern, western, and eastern Sierra, and from as far away as the upper watershed of the Colorado River, Cornell's notion of the advantages of constructing dry ground parks as emblematic of the Southern California landscape's ecological indigeneity is as compelling as it essential.

It does not reduce Cornell's powerful claims to know that he himself never fully developed the native landscapes he had proposed.

Perhaps closest to the idealized landscape he had promoted 1912 was his design work in the 1920s for what today is Torrey Pines State Park in San Diego. Its eponymous and signature tree, *Pinus torreyana,* is a rare, endangered species found only in the sandy bluffs and canyons of San Diego County and in a small grove on Santa Rosa Island, one of the Channel Islands off the Southern California Coast. The area was home ground of the Kumeyaay, whom the Spanish missionized, and whom later Mexicans and even later Americans forced out into the desert. By the mid- to late-nineteenth century, the windswept coastal terrain and its sentinel-like trees, aptly dubbed Soledad Pines by the Spanish, came under development pressure as the booming city of San Diego sprawled outward. Such threats in the late 1880s sparked protests.

Dr. C. C. Parry, who is credited with identifying the Torrey pine as a species, encouraged the San Diego Society of Natural History to take up this flag-waving opportunity. "Why should not San Diego, within whose corporate limits this straggling remnant of a past age finds a last, lingering resting place," and to dedicate this landscape "forever to the cause of scientific instruction and recreation"? Botanist J. G. Lemmon of the California State Board of Forestry seconded the notion, noting the "mournful interest" the Torrey pine generated, given that "there are but few trees of it left." He and others pressed for its preservation, but it was not until developers began to plat the land, clear cut the groves, and build homes along the coast for the city's burgeoning middle and upper classes that philanthropist Ellen Browning Scripps stepped in.

Purchasing land to stay the axe, she also underwrote plans for protecting and making accessible the remaining acres of Torrey pines—and tapped Ralph Cornell to do the design work. He had returned to California in 1919 after earning his Masters in Landscape Architecture from Harvard and serving on the frontlines in World War I. When he tramped over the site in 1922, he reported how struck he was struck by its "distinctiveness," its "unusually attractive" quality. "It is picturesque, unique, colorful, and beautiful, with a combination of nearby sea and distant mountains that delights the eye and soothes the soul." Convinced that it was *sui generis,* "un-imitated," Cornell argued that it should be "so kept—true to itself, typical of nothing, for it requires many more than one of a thing to establish a type."

In his work, he collaborated closely with native-plant advocate Theodore Payne. An English transplant, Payne was convinced that local species of trees, plants, and flowers should form the basis of the new park's biota. Yet neither he nor Cornell wanted the new site to be turned into a botanical garden. Cornell strongly counseled against planting any oaks ("they do not belong here"), urged the maintenance of the "chaparral covered floor of the canyon," proposed trails that would keep people out of the most fragile habitat, and suggested the planting of cacti in spots where they already existed. Yet, he implored, "as always, employ RESTRAINT." As for the whole grounds, he emphasized that they must be "ZEALOUSLY GUARDED." (The capitalizations are his.)

Cornell felt no such managerial restraint when given the opportunity to work for the college from which he graduated, a space whose development he would oversee for more than fifty years. In the early 1920s, he helped turn Pomona's campus into a garden, a physical evocation of those high-brow eastern campuses its curriculum replicated, the design for the open space of Marston Quad is but one case in point. Cornell created beautiful greenswards and memorial gardens, dotted them with native and non-native trees, and filled in with plants that were considerably more water dependent than drought tolerant. His impress remains evident in the college's lushness, an emerald isle in a sea of concrete.

The gap between the ideal he once embraced and reality he constructed simply reinforces just how transformational Cornell's original idea for a "genuine" Southern California palette, was — and remains.

Indigenous Grounds

2016

If you're tall enough, and I'm not, you could peer out of the large, north-facing, four-pane window in the Digital Humanities Studio on the third floor of Honnold Library in Claremont and gaze on a striking tableau. In the deep background are the chaparral-cloaked, rough folds of the San Gabriel foothills that rise up to Mount Baldy, the range's visual apex.

Pull your eyes down to the foreground and a different view comes into focus. You're looking at the Harvey S. Mudd Quadrangle, although few passersby see its fading metal name spelled out in concrete. They are on their way to somewhere else. Above that, what catches your vision are the towering stone pines and eucalyptuses, then a green sweep of lawn, establishing the x-and-y axis filled with other geometric shapes. Concrete sidewalks radiate out at right angles from the library connecting pedestrians to Dartmouth Avenue on the west. Stately Garrison Theater is to the immediate north, and to the east, McAllister Center, and Scripps and Claremont McKenna Colleges. Nothing is out of place. All grows according to plan. This built environment tightly structures the spatial dimensions of how we move through and experience it.

1901

Fast backward 115 years, a difficult act of imagination that historic photographs can stimulate. Consider a black-and-white photograph from the Claremont Colleges Digital Library, shot at the corner of what was then Warren (now College) Avenue and 7th Street, roughly a block south of Honnold Library. The mountains are vastly more prominent in this more unstructured terrain. The dirt road barely intrudes as your eye is caught first by the snow-capped high country. Filling the fore- and middle-ground is the alluvial fan that over the millennia has built up as floods roared out the canyons, carrying tons of debris—from boulders to fine grit—into the valley below.

The Tongva call this rough ground Torojoatngna, the Place Below Snowy Mountain. It was carpeted with an apparently untrammeled coastal sage ecosystem. In the flatlands, there was buckwheat, sages, ephemeral wildflowers, and grasses. The washes and creeks sustained oaks and sycamores. Rock-littered, with not a lot of shade, the landscape was open, capacious. There were even herds of pronghorn antelope. "We saw in the plain a very large drove of antelopes," wrote Fray Pedro Font in 1775, "which, as soon as they saw us, fled like the wind, looking like a cloud skimming along the earth."

Seemingly untrammeled, it was probably less pristine that it might seem. The Tongva and other Indigenous Peoples of Southern California used fire and other tools to manage resources that they wished to extract, including material they invested in their rituals and ceremonies, and that provided food and shelter. Notes biologist Paula M. Schiffman, "By manipulating the mix and abundance of native plant and animal species present in the ecosystem, the Tongva were able to exert control over the vertical structure of the region's vegetation and over a diversity of natural processes."

This indigenous landscape was more rapidly and enduringly modified when the Spanish and later Mexican settler-colonists ran vast herds of cattle, sheep, and goat in the inland valleys of Southern California. In 1817, Rancho San Rafael in the present-day San Gabriel Valley—a mere twenty miles to Claremont's west—had nearly two thousand cattle, hundreds of wild and tamed horses, and dozens of mules. Multiply those numbers across the region and it is little wonder these herbivores, in Schiffman's words, quickly became the "dominant organisms" that allowed them to "govern the region's ecological processes." Converting coastal sage into grassland, as happened in what is known now as the Pomona Valley in which Claremont is situated, was a reflection of their dominance.

Both the Indigenous and Spanish/Mexican settler-colonist managed landscapes in turn were buried beginning with the post-Civil War Americanization of the region. The late nineteenth-century arrival of the railroad, and the land speculation and town-building schemes that flowed in its wake, produced hardened roadbeds, gridded streetscapes, and a series of Victorian buildings that constituted the early campus of Pomona College. Since then, the Claremont Colleges, which now number seven institutions, have constructed an environment that signals its distance—historically, intellectually, even by the choice of which species to plant and where—from that earlier time and place. A plaque bolted in Pomona College's contemporary Smith Campus Center cheers the ecological conversion that had begun in the late 1880s and in which Ralph Cornell played a major role: "the clearing away of underbrush, and the planting of roses and other flowers about the building, with an oval lawn in front … forced back the jackrabbits and rattlesnakes."

2021

What would it take to reimagine the traces of that earlier biome? How might we peel back what the shovel dug in, the rake groomed, and the bulldozer flattened? How might we re-see what we have rendered invisible? To make the past, present?

Start with a trowel. It was the initial symbol of the student-led Ralph Cornell Society devoted to reengaging with the native plant palette that the Pomona alumnus once had extolled. In the early 2010s, the organization collaborated with the college Grounds Department to plant sage, deer grass, baccharis, and buckwheat in place of grass and other ground covers, a re-indigenizing that dovetailed with campus water-reduction commitments. The grounds department went farther, reintroducing the endemic Englemann oak, which had been logged out of the region by the early twentieth century. "It was very popular for lumber because it's a very straight oak tree," noted Kevin Quanstrom, grounds supervisor. "When going from nonnative to native plants, you're always going to save water because native plants tend to be dormant in the summertime. People should care—these trees were part of the ecosystem before we got here." Often on my morning walks, I'll swing through campus to pay my respects to some of the more than thirty trees that add to the biodiverse canopy. They are flourishing in their native soil.

These are small steps, to be sure, but they matter. Ethnobotanist and Tongva elder, the late Barbara Drake, made that case explicitly through her establishment of the Tongva Living History Garden, which has been an inspiration to many local students and faculty. Naomi Fraga, Director of Conservation at the California Botanic Garden in Claremont, has written extensively about why it is critical to repatriate endemic species "back into the landscape from which they grew."

These are among the influences—including a young Ralph Cornell—that led my wife and me to transform our quarter-acre suburban lot one mile west of campus. When we purchased the home in 2009, we ripped up the St. Augustine lawn, front and back, and with the help of landscapers began to reintroduce coastal sage biota. Initially, we planted bunches of deer grass as an evocative play on the now-departed sod; in the back, an Englemann oak. While lizards loved the cover the grass provided, few other species did. So, as a second draft, we thinned out the long-stemmed grass, and planted different varieties of ceanothus, bitterbush, and buckwheat, and a Channel Island poppy and cherry. Filling in the palette are large mounds of baccharis, manzanita, and different species of sage, along with sagebrush and California bay. Clematis and morning glory are inching up the wooden fence that frames the backyard, and even a prickly pear refugee has taken root. Someone had tossed a pad over the weathered fence, and I troweled it into place. It has now stretched up and out, catching the sun's rays.

On a recent afternoon, as I picked my way through the aromatic spring growth, jackrabbits and lizards scattered. An Anna's hummingbird, like a sewing machine, darted around a blue-flowered Cleveland sage, resting on a leaf while a pair of monarchs twirled into the air above, a mourning cloak. Chattering bushtits picked their way through oak and paperbark.

Home.

Book and cover design:
Dina Clark

Cover artwork and interior illustrations:
Sophie Wood Brinker

Editing:
Todd Shimoda

Publishing expertise:
Bruce Rutledge, Chin Music Press

Typefaces:
Adobe Garamond and Rialto

Paper:
Rolland Enviro Cover and Enviro Book,
100% recycled

Printer:
Imprimerie Gauvin

Informal consultant
(sharing opinions and enthusiasm
for books, typography and design):
Jim Faris